W9-CKP-699

# BREW YOUR OWN
# REAL ALE AT HOME

*Graham Wheeler and Roger Protz*

More than one hundred recipes based on famous
commercial brands of cask-conditioned beer

**BOOKS**

**The equipment needed to brew real ale at home**

# CONTENTS

Authors: Graham Wheeler and Roger Protz

Typeset by T & O Graphics, Broome, Bungay, Suffolk
Printed by WSOY, Finland

Published by CAMRA, The Campaign for Real Ale, 34 Alma Road, St Albans, Herts AL1 3BW

© CAMRA Ltd 1993
Reprinted 1993, 1994
ISBN 1.85249.113.2

Conditions of Sale:
This book shall not, by way of trade or otherwise, be lent, resold, hired out or otherwise circulated without the publisher's prior consent in any form of binding or cover other than in which it is published and without similar conditions being imposed on the subsequent purchaser. This book is published at a net price and supplied to the Publishers Association Standard Conditions of Sale registered under the Restrictive Trade Practices Act 1956. All rights reserved. No parts of this publication may be reproduced, stored in retrieval systems, or transmitted in any form or by any means electronic, mechanical, photocopying or otherwise, without the prior permission of CAMRA Limited.

# Introduction

I am to home brewing what Attila the Hun was to land reclamation. Show me a yeast cell and it dies. Confront me with a hop and it withers. Let me approach within sniffing distance of an ear of barley and it refuses to sprout. Reduce home brewing to its simplest form and the end product defiantly cocks a snook at me and refuses to drop bright or become drinkable.

My admiration for the likes of Graham Wheeler is boundless. He is able to produce gallons of high quality ale that match anything you can buy in a pub and at a fraction of the price. Unlike professional brewers, many of whom seem to have been trained by MI5 or the CIA, he is willing to pass on his skills and recipes to anyone willing to buy his books. And his finished results are not hit-and-miss but come from years of patient work in his kitchen and on his computer.

I have been writing about beer and brewing for more than seventeen years; in that time home brewing has waxed, waned and then waxed a second time. In the late 1970s and early 1980s, millions, myself included, took cans of sticky goo and sachets of ill-disguised baker's yeast and beavered away to produce "beers" that tasted like liquid Mother's Pride.

That mass market declined as more and more good, drinkable, commercial, cask-conditioned beers – real ales – came on to the market thanks to CAMRA's efforts. But now there is a small resurgence of interest in home brewing as the commercial brewers' greed and the recession drive all but the super-rich out of the pubs. But home brewing has changed; fewer people are doing it but they are doing it properly, refusing to cut corners and choosing to mash and boil, ferment and condition in the approved fashion.

I have a walk-on part in this book. My major effort was made elsewhere in compiling its companion, *The Real Ale Drinker's Almanac*. The springboard for that book was my belief that drinkers have a right to know what goes into their hard-earned pints. In the mid to late 1980s and starting in the United States, a movement developed that expressed concern about the doubtful ingredients used by some major brewers. I started to investigate the dodgy methods and cost-cutting cheap cereals and chemicals employed by giant brewing conglomerates, though I was relieved to find that these practices were confined mainly to the production of third rate quasi lagers and keg bitters. However, that led me to look more closely at the way in which real ales are made, not so much to question their ingredients, though they should not escape the spotlight, but to examine the recipes and brewing styles, in order better to inform the drinking public of the multitude of aromas and flavours to be savoured and enjoyed. I do not for one moment think that top fermented ales are better than genuine lager beers (several lagers would be on my bibulous desert island) but there is no doubt that top fermentation produces splendidly fruity and characterful beers that have been under-appreciated in Britain.

Brewers are reluctant to reveal their recipes, just as when, sixteen years ago, they refused to reveal their original gravities to CAMRA's *Good Beer*

1

*Guide.* Now, every brewer cheerfully lists his OGs and his ABVs, but is still chary of saying too much about recipes, oblivious to the fact that by the end of the century consumer protection legislation will almost certainly force him to do so.

It has taken three editions of the *Almanac* to wheedle some indication of recipes from most of the brewers. Bass at last has divulged some of its secrets. Among the regionals, Wolverhampton and Dudley still kept a tight zipper on the collective mouth for years but has now come clean. As Graham Wheeler points out, not even the most relaxed brewer has told me everything about what goes into his mash tun, copper, FV or cask, but some remarkable information has dribbled out, including details of such astonishingly large amounts of sugar being used in some beers that I will never again feel ashamed of pouring Tate & Lyle into my home brew; with a bit of luck and a fair wind, it might end up tasting like Marston's Pedigree.

The information gleaned from the brewers points up the amazing diversity of flavours within beer styles. A bitter made from 96 per cent pale and crystal malt will have a rich fruitiness while Pedigree, despite its impressive gravity, is dangerously subtle as a result of the high level of glucose, allied to the remarkable yeast strain propagated in its wooden Union system.

Knowing the recipe undoubtedly increases the enjoyment of drinking. When I first tasted Greene King's Rayment's Special Bitter, I thought it was remarkably like a Scottish "heavy" with a pronounced roast malt character. When Greene King released the recipe, for the *Almanac*, lo and behold, there was a good dash of roast in it. My "tutored tongue" had not failed me!

The aim of the *Almanac* is to encourage beer lovers to use their noses and their taste-buds as well as their throats. For too long good ale was tossed down the gullet without the drinker appreciating the complexity of aromas and flavours that made up his pint. Now a growing number of imbibers is sniffing and swirling, sucking and puckering. Many can spot a Fuggle and a Golding on the aroma and detect a generous dash of nutty crystal or chocolatey, dark malt on the palate. We are also discovering that, thanks to the workings of ale yeasts, some wonderful esters, ranging from light citric fruit to great wafts of pineapple, enrich light bitters and powerful old ales. And if the beer in your pub tastes remarkably like breakfast cereal, you will know that the brewer has gone a bit heavy on the torrefied wheat.

Now you can match your skills with those of the commercial brewers. Your finished beers may not quite match theirs but you will get enormous pleasure from making them and comparing them. You will also learn a great deal of brewing history, thanks to Graham's tireless devotion to his craft and his teasing out the methods of brewers centuries ago. I have gleaned much from his text that will better inform my future beer safaris.

So good brewing, good tasting and good drinking. And if sufficient numbers of you buy this book, Graham and I will be able to open our own home-brew pub – called, of course, The Attila the Hun.

**Roger Protz**

# 1 About this book

*There is a nice old-fashioned room at the "Rose and Crown" where bargees and their wives sit of an evening drinking their supper beer, and toasting their supper cheese at a glowing basketful of coals that sticks out into the room under a great hooded chimney and is warmer and prettier and more comforting than any other fireplace I ever saw. There was a pleasant party of barge people round the fire. You might not have thought it pleasant, but they did; for they were all friends or acquaintances, and they liked the same sort of things, and talked the same sort of talk. This is the real secret of pleasant society.*

*- E. Nesbit, The Railway Children, 1906*

I am a great lover of the institution known as the British Pub, and to me, Edith Nesbit's description embodies all that a pub should be. The fact that someone is a home brewer does not mean that he does not spend some considerable time in his local pub. Every home brewer has an idea of what his ideal beer should be, and he probably has a commercial beer in mind as the prototype. The easiest way of communicating the idea of a particular flavour or style of a beer is to equate it to a well-known commercial brand, and that is what this book is all about. It is a collection of over one hundred beer recipes which attempt to emulate commercially-brewed British beers.

The words *attempt* and *emulate* are used deliberately because few, if any, of the recipes included herein will be exact duplicates, despite the fact that they are based upon information supplied by the breweries to Roger Protz for his book *The Real Ale Drinker's Almanac*. Some breweries were more forthcoming than others, but very few provided sufficient information to generate exact duplicates of their recipes, particularly where hops are concerned, which is a bit of a black art anyway. No brewer's recipe is ever fixed; there are always minor adjustments being made to maintain consistent flavour and colour. Hops are a particularly variable commodity; brewers are constantly blending hops of different ages, different sources, different levels of bitterness, different varieties and in differing proportions in order to maintain consistency.

Many breweries were totally open about their ingredients and methods. Some breweries merely listed the ingredients without any indication of the respective ratios; while others conveniently forgot to include, or used euphemisms to describe, their copper sugars, syrups, caramel or any other ingredient which they felt may reflect badly upon them. Some brewers simply do not want the whole world to know their recipes; every brewer considers his recipe to be the best in the country, and many consider it to be his proprietary secret. The proprietor of a well-known Hampshire brewery once said to me, "Surely a brewer must be allowed some secrets, he shouldn't be expected to give his craft and possibly his livelihood away to anyone who cares to ask for it". I must confess that, despite my writing this particular book, I wholeheartedly agree with those sentiments.

As a consequence there is a considerable amount of computer-aided guesswork in these recipes, but they are as close as we will be able to get without a good deal of trial brewing and a multitude of comparisons on each individual beer. Each recipe is based upon the ingredients that the brewers have specified. The recipes have not been altered simply to make use of the ingredients that are currently available via the home brew trade; the trade will quite happily supply all of the ingredients we want, provided that there is demand for them. I have, however, made the occasional substitution for an obscure variety of hop, and in some cases minor additions of dark malts have been made to provide colour when the breweries concerned have used caramel or black invert sugar. In some cases sugars have been added to the recipe when the computer has felt that the brewer has "accidentally" forgotten to include them in his information. Yes, folks, the author of this book is really a computer!

This book came about by public demand after the publication of my book *Home Brewing – the CAMRA guide*. I had decided that I was never going to write another book. It was hard work writing the first one, and even harder work to get the thing published. However, in time my attitude mellowed and I was quite pleased with the way my book was received within the hobby. Eventually, on a visit to The Home Brew Shop in Farnborough the persuasive charm of Diane Green, and the enthusiasm of her husband Danny finally convinced me to have a go at it. To paraphrase Spike Milligan, "I said that I was never going to write another book – well, this is it!"

It is a lot quicker and easier to get a book like this on the road if you pinch someone else's research; which is exactly what I did. It saves an awful lot of time, effort, and several hundred postage stamps. So here it is, a joint venture. Roger Protz did the research, which means he sweet-talked or bullied the breweries into providing information about their beers. I wrote a computer programme to analyse the ingredients and turn them into the home-brew equivalent. I also wrote most of the auxiliary text which surrounds the recipes. The tasting notes at the head of each recipe are Roger's. Roger has had his palate profiled at a brewing laboratory, and as this sounds like a quite painful experience, I reasoned that it would be far better to leave the tasting to someone who already has the proper shaped tongue for the job. The tasting notes refer to the commercial varieties, by the way.

Although this book is written to cater for all kinds of brewer at all levels of experience, it does make the assumption that the reader has done some brewing before, even if only from beer kits. A certain amount of experience should be gained before attempting to emulate a commercial beer. There are several recipes (marked by an asterisk in the index) which are suitable for basic brewing using malt extract; these should be quite suitable for beginners, or anyone who prefers to brew from malt extract.

This book has been much improved through the endeavours of my good friend Kevin McCormack, the most enthusiastic grain brewer that I know. Kevin began home brewing when he was looking for something to occupy

4

his time upon retirement. He purchased a copy of my first book *Home Brewing* and within a year he had brewed all of the grain recipes in the book several times over. This put Kevin in the unique position of being able to point out to me any difficulties that he experienced while learning to brew using my first book. His comments in this direction were invaluable.

This, my second book, has had a chequered history. The original publisher went bust a few weeks before it was due to be printed, which, although unfortunate for the publisher and annoying to me, turned out for the better. I had previously given Kevin an early manuscript for the book and he, with unbounded enthusiasm, read it from cover to cover several times and ploughed his way through a surprising number of the recipes. The delay in publishing has provided me with the opportunity to incorporate his findings and suggestions, and my own rethinks; the result being that most of the up-cocks, wuddled murds, and other Wheelerisms have been eliminated. The recipes have been more fully tested than would otherwise have been possible. A better book is the result. Thanks Kevin.

I would like to thank the commercial brewing industry whose selfless assistance to the competition – the home brewing hobby – made this, and many other home brewing books possible. Thanks to Roger Protz for allowing me to filch his research. Again I am indebted to those wonderful people down at English Hops Ltd, particularly David Gardner, Director of Technical Services, who painstakingly told me all we need to know about EBUs. Many thanks to the directors of Ritchie Products for supporting my writing endeavours.

Up-to-date product information is a distinct advantage when you are trying to write an up-to-date brewing book. Therefore I would like to send my family coat of arms (two digits rampant) to the one or two manufacturers in the home-brew market place, who did not reply to my letters requesting information on their products.

Wassail!
**Graham Wheeler**

# 2 Home Brewing Methods

*Cenosilicaphobia – The fear of an empty glass*                    *Anon*

The main ingredient of beer is malted barley, often simply called malt. As home brewers we can either buy the malt as **grain** and brew **fully mashed** beers from this, or we can use **malt extract**, a gooey substance which comes in cans.

**Malt extract brewing** – no mash

Malt extract is a convenience tool. It knocks about three hours off the brewing process. Malt extract will produce convenient, palatable beers, but the beers will not compete with a full mash beer in a competition. In its simplest form no mash is required; all of the ingredients are simply boiled vigorously for an hour and a half and then strained into the fermentation bin. Unfortunately, when brewing by this method, one is restricted regarding the range of ingredients that can be employed. Only those ingredients which do not require enzymic conversion can be used, namely, crystal malt, black malt, roast barley; plus, of course, pale malt, which the malt extract replaces. The complete range of brewing sugars and syrups can also be used.

A selection of recipes is provided which are suitable for brewing using this method. Instructions are provided on page 39 – Brewing Instructions – method A.

**Malt extract brewing** – partial mash

This is a more advanced method of brewing from malt extract, which is a bit more difficult, but enables the complete range of brewing ingredients to be employed. A special type of malt extract is available, known as diastatic malt extract, the best known being EDME DMS. This type of extract contains the diastatic enzymes which are required to convert brewing adjuncts, such as wheat flour, flaked barley, flaked wheat, torrefied barley, etc into fermentable sugars. These enzymes are normally contributed by the pale malt, which the malt extract replaces. Partial mashing is simpler than full mashing; no mash tun is required and all of the ingredients can be contained in the boiler. The boiler temperature is raised to 67°C and held there for 45 minutes before being raised to the boil.

A selection of recipes is provided which are suitable for brewing using this method. Instructions are provided on page 41 – Brewing Instructions – method B.

**Fully mashed beers**

With a fully mashed beer we produce the fermentable sugars from crushed malted barley grain. Mashing from grain requires more equipment than extract brewing; a mash tun, or at least a grain bag will be required. It also requires more care, attention and skill. There is more opportunity for a mistake to be made, and it will take about a day to prepare a brew. Nevertheless it is well worth the effort. Only by brewing from grain can the best quality beers be produced, and it is the best way of closely emulating the commercial recipes contained herein. Mashing produces distinctive quality beers, and is the only technique which gives the brewer complete and flexible control over his product.

All of the recipes in this book can be brewed using this method. Instructions are provided on page 43 – Brewing Instructions – method C.

## Novice's notes

If you are a beginner there probably is little to be gained from reading this book, or any home brewing book for that matter, by starting at the beginning and reading it through to the end as if it were a novel. The easiest beers to brew in this book are those which are brewed using "Malt Extract Brewing Method A". To brew using this method you should go straight to page 39 and read the instructions for "Method A". If you understand the instructions you are ready to brew. You can return to the main body of the text if you want enlightenment on specific points. If you do not fully understand something, do not let it worry you unduly. The best way of learning is by doing.

If you have never brewed before it might be a good idea to gain some basic experience by using a beer kit. Choose a high quality (3kg) beer kit. They are much more reliable and produce much better beer than the cheaper 1.5kg and 1.8kg kits that are on the market.

# 3  Fermentable Ingredients

*ol heitir me(eth) mannum en me(eth) Assum bjorr*
*Ale it is called among men, and among Gods beer*
*(Old Norse from the Alvismal c950)*

\* \* \*

*He ne drinc(eth) win ne be'or*
*(Luke 1.15, Lindisfarne Gospels, c1100)*

## Barley

The first quotation at the heading to this chapter is the first ever recorded mention of the word **ale**; the second quotation is the first recorded mention of the word *beer* as an *alcoholic* beverage in the English language. It is amusing to learn that, as we do today, the Vikings were struggling with the distinction between ale and beer over 1000 years ago. However, the quotation was probably somewhat facetious. The Vikings considered themselves Gods, and they called their drink beer, whereas the British were mere mortals and they called their drink ale.

In any language the word beer is derived from the word for barley, which in Old English is *baerlic*. This became shortened and mutated into *bear* and *bere* in the days when spelling was optional. Indeed, the name of the English town Bere Regis refers to the quality of the barley that was grown there. However, the fact remains that beer and barley are synonymous and the primary ingredient of the beverage is barley, malted barley to be precise.

Malted barley is barley which has been soaked in water and allowed to germinate. When germination has proceeded far enough, germination is halted by drying the malt. It is then kilned to ensure that the malt is dried properly and brought to the desired colour.

### Malts for brewing

### Pale malt (colour 5 EBC)
This is the primary ingredient of most English beers. This is simply malted barley, lightly kilned during drying to provide a very light colour. Pale malt can be purchased whole or crushed; it must be crushed before use in the mash tun.

### Mild ale malt (colour 7 EBC)
Mild ale malt is made from higher nitrogen barley than pale malt. This allows it to be kilned to a darker colour than pale malt without reducing its diastatic activity. The diastatic activity of mild ale malt is, in fact, higher than pale malt, but at the expense of extract. A high level of diastatic activity is required in order to assist in the conversion of the high levels of adjuncts

8

which are typical of mild ales. Mild ale malt can be purchased whole or crushed; it must be crushed before use in the mash tun.

## Amber malt (colour 40-60 EBC)
Amber malt is made by kilning mild ale malt at 100-150°C until the desired amber colour is reached. It is then removed from the kiln and allowed to cool. It provides a biscuit flavour and a rich golden colour to beers. Amber malt can be purchased whole or crushed; it must be crushed before use in the mash tun.

## Chocolate malt (colour 900-1200 EBC)
Chocolate malt is a malt that has been kilned to a very dark colour. It is used to provide flavour and colour to dark beers: milds, stouts and porters. Chocolate malt can be purchased whole or crushed; it must be crushed before use in the mash tun.

## Black malt (colour 1250-1500 EBC)
Black malt, as its name implies, is malted barley that has been kilned to a high degree, turning the malt black. It is used for flavour and colour. Black malt does not need to mashed. It is used in the mash tun for convenience, but it can be used in the copper when brewing from malt extract.

## Roasted barley (colour 1000-1550 EBC)
Roasted barley is unmalted barley that has been roasted until it is black. It is used to impart a unique dry, burnt flavour to stouts. Being unmalted it is rich in beta glucans and other head enhancing components, and its use promotes a thick Guinness-style head. Roasted barley does not need to mashed; it is used in the mash tun for convenience, but it can be used in the copper when brewing from malt extract.

## Crystal malt (colour 100-300 EBC)
Crystal malt is made in a factory, by wetting high nitrogen malt and holding it at 65°C for a while in an enclosed vessel. The grains are then dried at 250°C. Crystal malt does not need to be mashed; it is used in the mash tun for convenience, but it can be used in the copper when brewing from malt extract.

## Wheat malt
Wheat malt is an increasingly popular ingredient in British beers. It supplies a unique flavour and improves head retention.

## Cereal adjuncts

## Wheat flour
Brewer's wheat flour was, until recently, the most common adjunct used by breweries in this country. Most breweries used about 5 per cent in their

grist make up. Being unmalted its main property is to improve head retention, but it also acts as a nitrogen dilutant producing beers of less haze potential. Wheat flour has, in fact, been used for centuries, but for different reasons. Brewers of old used it as a yeast food by sprinkling it on to the surface of the fermenting wort after the first yeast skimming, but that was probably misguided.

Brewer's wheat flour has a controlled protein level of around 7 per cent. A certain amount of protein is necessary in order to yield glycoproteins, which aid head retention, but too much protein will affect shelf life and clarity. Therefore, brewer's wheat flour is made from varieties of soft wheat, which are rich in glycoproteins but low in other nitrogenous substances. The wheat is milled to a controlled particle size and then classified in an air centrifuge which separates a proportion which has the correct protein level. The requirements for brewer's wheat flour are quite different from baker's wheat flour.

While this book was being written, the only manufacturer of brewer's wheat flour suddenly announced that it was going to stop making it. As a result many brewers have changed to torrefied wheat or flaked wheat, but some brewers still claim to use wheat flour. Where wheat flour is called for in a recipe, and if your homebrew shop does not have proper brewers' wheat flour, then substitute the same quantity of flaked wheat or torrefied wheat, or you may wish to try plain domestic flour.

### Torrefied wheat, Flaked wheat, Flaked maize, Flaked barley

These are other adjuncts which are commonly used in British beers, particularly mild ales. Obviously, they all impart subtly different flavours and characteristics to the beers.

### Sugars

All brewing sugars and special syrups are known as *copper sugars,* or *copper syrups* because they are added to the copper during the boil. They do not need mashing and are not added to the mash tun. They can be used with equal success in grain brewing or malt extract brewing.

Commercial brewers have a bewildering array of brewing sugars available to them. The sugars are derived from a number of sources, have varying degrees of fermentability and come in various colours. There are a number of homebrew products available in powder, liquid and sticky-chip form that are spuriously labelled "brewing sugar", "glucose" or some other non-committal term. Very often it is not clear from the label what the product actually is; it could be one of a dozen different forms of sugar. Ideally the label should specify the type of sugar, its fermentability and its EBC colour rating, so that there can be no confusion. All of these parameters are freely available from the primary manufacturers so there is no hardship involved in printing them on home brewing product labels.

## Invert cane sugar

Brewers rarely use ordinary cane sugar, but instead use *invert* cane sugar. Cane sugar (sucrose) consists of equal parts of glucose and fructose which are bonded together molecularly. Yeast can secrete an enzyme (invertase) which breaks these molecular bonds and splits the sugar into its two component types. Yeast needs to break these bonds before it can ferment the sugars. Invert cane sugar is sucrose which has had the molecular bonds already broken by an industrial process, which saves the yeast doing it for itself. Ordinary cane sugar can be used in place of invert with no apparent difference to the home brewer, except perhaps in colour. Brewers have traditionally used invert sugar because they feel that ordinary sugar gives a "sugar tang" to the finished beer, and causes disproportionate hangovers. Whether or not this is true is a matter of conjecture, but I can believe it.

Invert sugar can be in the form of sticky blocks, chunks, or syrup. It is available to commercial brewers in four colours from No. 1 to No. 4, No. 1 being the lightest and No. 4 being almost black. Invert sugar, like ordinary sugar, is 100 per cent fermentable and leaves no residual sweetness or body in a beer. Tate & Lyle Golden Syrup is invert sugar.

When invert sugar is called for in any recipe, household cane sugar can be used instead.

## Maize syrups (glucose syrups/maltose syrups)

These syrups are derived from maize (corn) and they come in two basic types: high glucose and high maltose. It is not terribly important which type is used, since the end result is about the same. The important fact is that these syrups, unlike pure glucose, are not 100 per cent fermentable. They contain about 20 per cent non-fermentable sugars and therefore do not dry and thin the beer as much as cane sugar or pure glucose would. Glucose chips are the same product in solidified form and can be used just as well.

Both the syrups and the chips are available through homebrew sources, but the labelling on these products often leaves a lot to be desired, and it is quite possible that you could end up with the wrong stuff. Unfortunately, "glucose" has become a very euphemistic term and is used incorrectly to describe a whole range of sugars in both the food and brewing industries.

In the recipes the terms "maltose syrup" and "glucose syrup" refer to maize derived syrups. For home brewing purposes it matters not whether high maltose or high glucose syrup is used, the end result is about the same. However, home brew packagers simply call this stuff "liquid brewing sugar"; which can mean anything. When buying it try to ensure that it is a maize-derived sugar.

## Caramel

Caramel is a colouring agent derived from burnt sugar. Some commercial brewers have a habit of throwing caramel into their beers for the sole purpose of making one beer look like a beer of a different type. My opinion on this pernicious practice is well known to those who have read my other ramblings on the subject. However, if every commercial brewer who used caramel were excluded from this book, it would be a very slim volume indeed! I do not object to caramel being used to make minor colour adjustments to a beer. Unfortunately, many people drink with their eyes and not their mouths, therefore many brewers use caramel to maintain colour consistency in their beers.

Recent EC restrictions on the use of caramel are being phased in, and most breweries are being forced to cut back on the use of the stuff; some are even getting around to brewing their beers properly! There are new substitutes for brewer's caramel, and these will undoubtedly be used for colouring beer. Should you need to colour your beer some home-brew shops stock brewer's caramel. Liquid gravy browning is caramel, and can be used in an emergency.

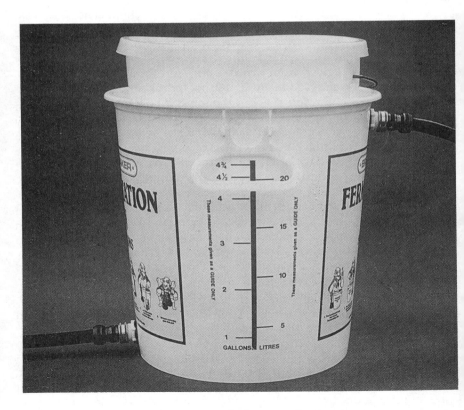

**A mash tun made from two buckets**

12

# 4 Hops

*He made for the cellar door, and presently reappeared, somewhat dusty, but with a bottle of beer in each paw and another under each arm. "Self-indulgent beggar you seem to be Mole," he observed. "Deny yourself nothing" ...The Rat, meanwhile, was busy examining the label on one of the beer bottles. "I perceive this to be Old Burton," he remarked approvingly. "Sensible Mole! The very thing! Now we shall be able to mull some ale! Get the things ready, Mole, while I draw the corks."*

*- Kenneth Grahame, Wind In The Willows*

The varieties and relative quantities of hops employed determines the predominant characteristics of any particular beer. There are a couple of dozen different varieties of hops available which can be used in any combination and quantity. The possibilities are endless. The hop characteristic of a beer is the most difficult aspect to emulate, and provides the most variable aspect of beer production. Hops are also the ingredients of the most variable quality. Not only does hop flavour mellow with age, but the same variety of hop grown in another region will be subtly different. Not only do hops provide bitterness but they also supply aroma and flavour in varying degrees, and they can be used at several different stages of the brewing process to impart different characteristics.

## Bittering hops (copper hops)
Bittering hops are those which are put into the copper at the beginning of the boil for bittering and preservation purposes. Alpha acid is the primary bittering ingredient of a hop, and it follows that high alpha hops are the most economical copper hops, although any variety of hop can be used for bittering purposes. Indeed, high alpha acid hops often give a degree of harshness, whereas the highest quality beers use low alpha hops for bittering such as Fuggles and Golding, which are much more mellow.

High alpha hops are usually hybrids, bred specially for high alpha acid content and high yields in the hop garden. The high yields make them cheaper to buy and their high alpha acid content make them economical to use in the copper. The most common bittering hop used in this country is Target, but its bittering is harsh and so it is often blended with other varieties.

High alpha hops usually have a harsh flavour and a poor aroma. In fact, the higher the alpha acid content of the hop, the poorer its flavour and aroma becomes. This is not considered to be terribly important by many breweries because much of the flavour and aroma content of the hop is driven off during the boil, although the bittering remains.

It is conventional to restore these lost components by adding a quantity of *"aroma hops"* to the copper during the last fifteen or twenty minutes of the boil. This is known as *"late hopping"* and a quantity of high quality aroma hops, equivalent to about 20 per cent of the main batch, is usually employed. Late hops do not contribute much bitterness to the brew because the short boiling period that they receive does not give enough time for much of the bitterness to be extracted.

### Aroma hops
Aroma hops are those varieties of hop that are considered to have a fine flavour and aroma. Although aroma hops can be used as bittering hops, and the best quality beers employ aroma hops for bittering, they are low in alpha acid and yield. They are therefore more expensive to use as such. In general, aroma hops are usually employed as late hops, being added to the copper in the last fifteen minutes of the boil, or as dry hops added to the cask after filling.

Goldings and Fuggles are considered to be the finest aroma hops, but they have low yields, low alpha acid and low disease resistance, and are therefore more expensive. Many breweries use the new general purpose hops for all or part of their aroma. However, the hop growers claim that **all** of the hybrid varieties of hop, with the possible exception of Target, have a pleasing aroma, but that is a matter of opinion! Mind you, Ind Coope Benskin's Bitter and Taylor Walker Bitter are both late hopped and dry hopped with Target. 'Nough said.

### General purpose hops
These are new hybrid varieties which have been developed specially for high yields and disease resistance, but which have a moderate alpha acid content and a sufficiently delicate aroma to be used as a copper hop or aroma hop. It is a case of being jack of all trades, master of none.

Challenger is the most common general purpose hop used in this country, followed closely by Northdown. Northdown is a replacement for the old Northern Brewer varieties. Challenger and Northdown have the lowest alpha acid content of the new hybrid varieties, and I would suspect that these will eventually completely replace the traditional Goldings and Fuggles as aroma hops.

### Dry hopping
Dry hopping is the term used to describe the practice of adding a few hop cones to the cask after filling. This will add a hoppy aroma to the beer but does not add to the bitterness, or the hoppy flavour of a beer. Fuggles and Golding are the most common hops used for dry hopping.

### Using different varieties of hop
The varieties of hop used in the recipes contained in this book are, where possible, the varieties specified by the brewer concerned, and are not necessarily those which are commonly available in home-brew shops at the time of writing. It would be folly to write the recipes around the ingredients that happen to be available at the current time because the hobby would never progress any further than its current state and would therefore stagnate.

14

The range of hops available through homebrew wholesalers at the time of writing is fairly good, particularly when one considers that 99 per cent of all published recipes simply call for Goldings or Fuggles, or similar traditional varieties. In fact, the only glaring absence in my wholesaler's lists is Challenger, which only surprises me because it is Britain's second most widely grown hop. But you can rest assured that Challenger is bound to appear when a demand exists for it.

However, the fact remains that there are about 25 varieties of hop available in this country, many more if one takes regional variations into account, so it would be unfair to expect our shops to stock the whole range. There will be times when you will need to substitute one variety of hops for another, either because the specified hops are not in stock, or simply because you wish to experiment or use hops that you already have. Unfortunately, a direct weight-for-weight substitution will not provide the same level of bitterness, but a simple calculation will reveal the proper quantity of hops to use.

Assuming that you wish to maintain an equivalent level of bitterness, a simple comparison of the alpha acid ratios of the two hop varieties will provide the new quantity of hops. For example; if your recipe calls for 40 grams of Challenger, but you wish to use Goldings instead, the following simple relationship is all that is required.

$$\textit{multiplication factor} \quad = \quad \frac{\textit{Alpha acid of specified hops}}{\textit{Alpha acid of substitute hops}}$$

Challenger has an alpha acid of 7.7 per cent and Goldings have an alpha acid of 5.3 per cent. The sum then becomes:

$$= \quad \frac{7.7}{5.3} \quad = \quad 1.45$$

To obtain the new weight of hops simply multiply the quantity of the specified hops by the factor, thus:

$$\textit{new weight of hops} \quad = \quad 40 \times 1.45 \quad = \quad 58 \, \textit{grams}$$

Alternatively, using the same figures:

$$\textit{new weight of hops} \quad = \quad \frac{40 \times 7.7}{5.3} \quad = \quad 58 \, \textit{grams}$$

As a rule of thumb when experimenting with different varieties of hops, the low alpha acid varieties are considered to be the best quality hops, but they are less economical because more of them need to be used for a given level of bitterness. The economics of different varieties of hop are only of concern to the commercial brewers, and should not be of any consequence to home-brewers.

In general, the higher the alpha acid content of a hop, the higher its bittering power becomes, but its flavour becomes harsher and its aroma more objectionable. The lower the alpha acid content of a hop the lower its bittering power, but its flavour becomes more mellow, and its aroma more delicate.

The typical alpha acid content of the most common varieties of hops are listed below.

## Alpha acid table

| Variety | % Alpha Acid | Application |
| --- | --- | --- |
| Bramling Cross: | 6 | Aroma hop |
| British Columbian: | 7 | General purpose hop |
| Bullion: | 5.3 | General purpose hop |
| Challenger: | 7.7 | General purpose hop |
| Goldings: | 5.3 | Aroma hop |
| Fuggle: | 4.5 | Aroma hop |
| Hallertau: | 7.5 | Aroma hop |
| Northdown: | 8 | General purpose hop |
| Northern Brewer: | 7.6 | General purpose hop |
| Omega: | 9.7 | High bittering copper hop |
| Progress: | 6.2 | Aroma hop |
| Saaz: | 5.5 | Aroma hop |
| Styrian Goldings: | 7.9 | Aroma hop |
| Target: | 11.2 | High bittering copper hop |
| Whitbread Golding: | 6.3 | Aroma hop |
| Yeoman: | 10.6 | High bittering copper hop |
| Zenith: | 9 | High bittering copper hop |

## European Bittering Units (EBU)

European Bittering Units or, less insularly, International Bittering Units are a world standard method of assessing the bitterness of beers. Some breweries have provided information on the bitterness of their beers in terms of EBUs and this information has been useful in compiling the recipes. As the rest of the brewing world uses EBUs as an indication of bitterness, it seems appropriate that the homebrew hobby should follow suit.

The bitterness of a beer in EBUs is given by:

$$EBU = \frac{\textit{weight of hops} \times \textit{alpha acid of hops} \times \textit{utilisation}}{\textit{volume brewed} \times 10}$$

To find the weight of hops required in order to produce a given bitterness in a given volume of beer the formula can be rewritten thus:

$$Weight\ of\ hops = \frac{EBU \times 10 \times Volume\ brewed}{alpha\ acid \times utilisation}$$

Where: Volume is in litres
Weight of hops is in grams
Alpha acid of hops is in per cent
Hop utilisation is in per cent

## Hop utilisation

The hop utilisation figure in the equation corresponds to the efficiency of the boil and is dependent upon many things: the vigour of the boil, the length of the boil, the specific gravity of the wort, and the equipment used. In general the utilisation achieved will be in the range of 20-35 per cent under ideal conditions, with a vigorous 1½ hour boil and the hops boiling freely in the wort.

Because of the variations in methods and technique between home brewers, and the variations in quality of the hops available to us, I have assumed that a typical hop extraction efficiency experienced by home brewers will be at the lower end of this range; namely 20 per cent. All of the recipes in this book are calculated using this figure.

This simplifies the equation slightly. Rewriting it to incorporate 20 per cent extraction efficiency:

$$Weight\ of\ hops = \frac{EBU \times Volume\ brewed}{alpha\ acid \times 2}$$

Therefore to achieve 25 units of bitterness in 27 litres of beer using Golding hops at an alpha acid content of 5.3 per cent:

$$Weight\ of\ hops = \frac{22 \times 27}{5.3 \times 2} = 56\ grams$$

This assumes a minimum of a one-and-a-half hour boil, and a good vigorous boil.

The majority of home brewers boil their hops using a hop bag, as opposed to my preferred method of boiling them freely in the wort. Hop bags are available through the homebrew trade, whereas a home brewer would have to construct a hopback similar to mine. The employment of a hop bag during the boil will reduce utilisation efficiency. The quantities of hops specified in these recipes are considerably lower than is usual home brew practice. Home brewers do tend to use much higher hop rates than the commercial brewers do. The perceived bitterness of a beer is a subjective assessment, and such things cannot be quantified in a rigid mathematical manner. Brewers are continually jiggling their hop rates to maintain a consistent perceived bitterness.

EBUs apply only to the bittering hops, i.e. the hops that are put into the copper at the beginning of the boil. Late hops do not contribute much bitterness to the wort due to the shorter dwell time in the copper. They only restore aroma which has been lost in the boil.

Late hops are generally 20-25 per cent of the quantity of bittering hops employed and the exact amount is determined by experience and personal preference.

## Hop pellets

The major breweries tend to use hop pellets rather than whole hops. In fact, hop pellets account for more than 70 per cent of Britain's hop consumption, although they are not popular in the British home brewing hobby. Hop pellets are nothing other than whole hops which have been beaten to a powder and then compressed into pellets.

In a traditional brewery, i.e. a brewery that uses whole hops, the hops settle on to the perforated floor at the bottom of the hop back and act as a filter bed to filter out the trub and other undesirable matter generated by the boil. In this way spent hop debris and trub are left behind in the hop back, leaving a clear and bright wort. If these products are not removed and are carried across to the final beer, the trub will cause clarity and stability problems and the hop debris will develop a tannic bitter taste with age, caused by the woody strigs and other parts of the hop.

Hop pellets present a problem. They disintegrate during the boil and cannot act as a filter bed to filter out the trub. Also, the spent hop debris itself is difficult to filter out.

Commercial brewers who use hop pellets have an additional piece of equipment, known as a whirlpool, which removes the hop debris and trub. There is nothing particularly complicated about this apparatus; it is simply a cylindrical tank with tangential inlet and outlet pipes situated near the bottom. The tank is filled via the inlet pipe which, being tangential, sets the wort revolving in the manner of a whirlpool, hence its name. The trub and hop debris are drawn into the eye of the whirlpool and settle in a neat little pile in the centre of the vessel. The trub, being composed of gummy, sticky particles, stick nicely together and stay put. When sufficient time has elapsed for the debris to settle, usually half an hour to one hour, the clear wort is drawn off via the outlet, which maintains the slow spinning motion.

You can imitate the effect quite easily by putting a couple of teaspoons of tea leaves into a half-pint beer mug of cold water, or some other clear glass vessel with a broad flat bottom. Change the water a couple of times while retaining the tea leaves, so that the water is clear enough to see what is going on, then stand it on a flat surface and give it a brisk stir. Observe that when the water stops spinning the leaves end up in a neat pile in the centre of the mug. In fact it is not even necessary to give it a particularly brisk stir, the effect does not take place until the rotation has slowed below a certain critical speed, which is surprisingly low. It should be possible to emulate a whirlpool on a homebrew scale using a smooth sided fermentation bin. We could use a large wooden spoon to stir the thing into action. I may have a go at making one when I am not too busy writing about it.

Although I prefer to use whole hops and feel that they do a better job, I can nevertheless appreciate that the use of pellets can offer certain advantages to the home brewer and that some people may prefer to use them. Hop pellets are more stable in storage than whole hops and will probably give better utilisation efficiency in the home brew environment. The need for a hop back is also eliminated. The disadvantages are that the mechanical action of whole hops swirling around in the boiler is lost, there is no filter action for the trub and the possibility exists of undesirable tannin producing substances being carried over to the finished beer.

However, hop pellets can be used in home brewing provided that care is taken to ensure that as much trub and hop debris as possible are excluded from the final beer. After the boil, switch off the heat, cover the boiler with a lid of some sort and leave to stand for about half an hour or so for the trub and hop debris to settle on to the bottom. This will allow relatively clear wort to be drawn off for most of its volume. Draw off the wort via the tap and strain it through a fine nylon sieve into the collection vessel. The sieve will trap any seeds or other debris floating on the surface or in suspension. Tip the boiler gently to retrieve as much clear wort as possible via the tap. It does not matter if a bit of debris gets carried across, the sieve will catch most of it, and that which does get into the wort probably will not matter much.

A friend of mine boils three or four six-inch squares of muslin cloth with his wort when using hop pellets. Apparently the gummy trub adheres to the muslin and thereby removes it from the wort. The muslin is washed after the brewing session. I personally have not tried it yet, but it might be worth a try by the more experimentally minded.

# 5 Yeast

*Worts were pitched with four gallons of good yeast on Friday evening; on Saturday night at eleven o'clock had passed the worty change; roused her that same night, and at nine o'clock on Sunday morning; heat sixty eight degrees; the same Sunday afternoon at two o'clock; ditto at six o'clock the next morning; and at eleven o'clock at night. on Tuesday morning at six o'clock found her coming to her stomach, heat seventy-three degrees; skimmed her at eleven o'clock, and put in one pound of salt and two pounds of wheat flour; roused her well, and let her lay till one o'clock; skimmed her again and put in one pound of coriander seed; at five o'clock in the evening found her gravity but six pounds per barrel, and the heat seventy four degrees; cleansed into twenty-six barrels; filled up every three hours for eighteen hours; the ale worked in the casks for two days; stowed away twenty four barrels in all.*

*(From a brewer's journal for Kingston Ale, early 1800s)*

### Friendly fungi

There are not many life forms simpler than the humble yeast cell. It is a mere fungus or mould, yet it has probably provided some of the greatest services to mankind, and given more pleasure to the human race than almost anything else. Yeast supplied us with a safe and wholesome fluid to drink, in the form of ale and wine, in the days when the water supplies were unsafe; helped to make a cheap and wholesome food, in the form of bread, to fill hungry bellies. At one time ale and bread were considered to be the two major necessities of life, the staple diet of the populace. Our pet yeast was responsible for both.

Brewer's yeast is a rich source of B complex vitamins and ends up in all sorts of foods and medicines: Marmite, Bovril, Oxo, Bisto, Vetzymes and numerous vitamin supplements. Yeast can be used genetically to manufacture a number of medicines and antibodies. Indeed, one of its kin, a fungus called penicillum notatum, was responsible for the foundation of modern antibiotics, due its ability to generate bactericides which kill susceptible forms of bacteria, or at least inhibit their growth. Alas, there are no monuments erected to celebrate the part that the humble yeast has played in the development of mankind.

### Nature's alcoholics

Although we all know that yeast is responsible for the production of alcohol, it is important to know a little bit about the conditions that yeast requires in order to produce this minor miracle, if we are to have trouble free brewing.

When yeast is first pitched into our wort it needs to grow at a very fast rate in order to establish itself and form the yeasty head. In order to be able to do this it needs plenty of dissolved air in the wort, because yeast can only multiply significantly under *aerobic* conditions, i.e. in the presence of dissolved air.

When the yeast has multiplied sufficiently and used up all the dissolved air in the wort, it is forced to respire *anaerobically*, i.e. without air, then it begins to produce alcohol. It is only under *anaerobic* conditions that yeast produces alcohol.

This brings us to an important point that is often not made clear in home brewing books or in the instructions supplied with kits:

*At the time the yeast is pitched it is important that the wort is well aerated, but from that point on it is important that care is taken to ensure that a minimum of air comes into contact with the beer.*

The important boiling phase of our beer production drives off any dissolved air that may be present. It is therefore necessary for us to aerate the wort after it has cooled. The easiest way of doing this is to pour the wort slowly from one fermentation bin to another once or twice. I usually run the wort slowly via the tap. The wort should be cool before this is done because the solubility of oxygen is greater at low temperatures.

**Types of yeast**
There are a great many varieties of yeast used in brewing, but they all fit into one of two broad classifications: bottom working and top working.

Bottom working yeasts, *saccharomyces uvarum,* sometimes called lager yeasts, are those where most of the yeast settles to the bottom of the vessel during fermentation, although this effect may not be evident in the home brewing environment. The major characteristic of this type of yeast is that it will work at much lower temperatures than its top-working counterpart. It is used for Pilsner style lagers.

Top working yeasts, *saccharomyces cerevisae,* sometimes called ale yeasts, are those where most of the yeast rises to the surface of the wort during fermentation. It is the type of yeast used in all British-style beers, and most of the beers of Europe.

It is a truth that in order to emulate fully a particular brewery's beer, you will need to use the same type of yeast. However, a word of warning is in order here. Top working English Ale yeasts can be further classified into two broad sub-divisions which I have euphemistically termed "northern yeasts" and "southern yeasts", although the geographical distinction is not particularly apparent these days.

Northern yeasts are those which are common in the north of England, Yorkshire in particular, but can also be found in Manchester and other areas. Without going too deeply into the technicalities of the subject, northern yeasts do not particularly enjoy making alcohol and need frequent "rousing" to maintain fermentation. That is, every few hours the yeast head needs to be stirred back into the wort. Some types require frequent aeration as well, and as a consequence they produce copious amounts of surplus yeast which needs to be constantly removed. A unique fermentation vessel known as a "Yorkshire Stone Square", now almost extinct, evolved to cope with this style of yeast. A Yorkshire Square needs attention every two hours. Modern breweries that use northern yeast keep the yeast active by continuously pumping the wort from the bottom of the fermentation vessel and spraying it back in at the top. This keeps the wort circulating through the yeast head, which is effectively what a Yorkshire Stone Square did. The risk of infection from airborne bacteria is high.

Northern style yeasts would be quite troublesome in the homebrew environment. We normally would neither have the time to attend to our fermentation every few hours for five or six days, nor the skills required to build special fermentation equipment to cope. A home brewer would be best advised to stick to southern style yeasts, irrespective of the style of beer that he is intending to brew.

Southern style yeasts are better adapted for use in ordinary open vessels, are much less troublesome, and can be left to get on with their work unattended. They should not need rousing and certainly would not need re-aeration under normal circumstances. The English Ale yeasts supplied to the homebrew trade would be southern style yeast, often Whitbread strain B, which is quite a vigorous hard worker. But, if you do happen to have access to real live brewer's yeast from a brewery, this point should be borne in mind.

## Yeast performance

A good, top working, English Ale yeast should quickly establish itself into a thick, dense, rocky head. This head should be 2-3 inches deep, have a density something like whipped cream, and look like something out of Quatermass. The term "rocky head" is an attempt to convey the impression of a thick, ragged, uneven surface of chunky appearance as opposed to a weak, self-levelling foam; although it may settle into a level mass towards the end of fermentation. It is difficult to describe or illustrate the effect precisely because the appearance changes with differing conditions and during different stages of fermentation; indeed every head is different, and could be considered an art form. However, the description should be adequate to give you the general idea of things, and if you achieve something close to it, your yeast is performing well.

If you are using high quality ingredients, use a yeast starter solution and aerate your wort before, or just after, pitching the yeast you will achieve good yeast performance. If you do not, then the first thing to blame is the yeast itself. However, yeast is fickle stuff, and it is not always fair to blame the suppliers.

Other requirements of a good yeast is that it clears down quickly and unaided after barrelling. If you bottle your beers, a type of yeast that packs down firmly and adheres to the bottom of the bottles as a film would be an advantage. Guinness yeast behaves in this manner, which is why many home brewers prefer it. Some yeasts collect as a loose clump at the bottom of the bottle and require more care when pouring.

## Fermentation temperature

The fermentation temperature for an ale, using a proper ale yeast, should be maintained between about 18 and 22°C; optimum 20°C. If you are fermenting in a shed or garage during winter when the ambient air temperature is low, then a higher fermentation temperature may be beneficial; perhaps as high as 24°C. The trick is to maintain the lowest temperature at which the yeast functions properly. Too low a temperature and the yeast head may drop into the beer; too high a temperature and off-flavours may result. Fermentation heaters are available in homebrew shops; these are invaluable during cold weather.

In order to ensure that the yeast head is rapidly formed, it is usually beneficial to pitch the yeast when the wort temperature is relatively high, between 25 and 30°C, and allow the temperature to drop to a more appropriate fermentation temperature when the head has formed.

**Packaged yeasts**
I have always mistrusted packaged yeasts. In my early days of home brewing I began using packaged yeasts and had several problems with weak fermentation and poor yeast performance. Eventually I began to propagate my own yeasts, one pinched from a Guinness bottle, and another obtained from a local brewery. I have had no trouble since. However, those were early days, although not many years ago. Not only did the drying techniques of the time kill most of the yeast, but little importance was placed upon yeast quality. Some of the stuff supplied as brewer's yeasts were wine yeasts, and possibly even baker's yeast. It may have been a lager yeast if you were lucky, but rarely was it a proper ale yeast.

These days things have changed for the better. Drying techniques have improved giving higher viability and the industry genuinely attempts to supply good quality true-to-type packaged yeast to home brewers. However, it is still important to select yeast carefully. Many packaged yeasts are not true-to-type, top-working, English Ale yeasts and it is important to be able to read between the lines of the description on the yeast package if disappointment is to be avoided.

Try to avoid yeasts which are labelled in a non-committal manner. Packaged yeasts, which are simply described as "beer yeast", "brewer's yeast", or even "genuine brewer's yeast", are very often some nondescript general purpose yeast that is produced in a commercial yeast propagator. It is certainly not clear from the description whether it is supposed to be an ale yeast or a lager yeast. The Chambers dictionary defines "beer" as being made with a bottom-working yeast, and "ale" as being made with a top worker. Although this Chamber's definition may be questionable (there seems to be no common usage, historical, or even etymological precedence for this definition), it is safest to assume that a package labelled "beer yeast" is a bottom-worker. It is hard to believe, but true, that the British homebrew industry finds it easier and cheaper to obtain continental lager yeasts than it does English ale yeasts.

The anonymous little packets that come with most beer kits should be thrown away immediately. The beer kit manufacturers are of the opinion that their market is price driven as opposed to quality driven, and the yeast supplied with some of the kits is of very dubious origin.

If you wish to brew "real ale" then it is important to obtain "real yeast". A packet labelled with a description such as: *real ale*", "*English ale*", "*ale*" or even, "*English beer*" is rather more specific than a non-committal "brewer's yeast", and is far more likely to contain a strain of yeast appropriate to the type of beer that you intend to brew. Although, sadly, even that cannot be guaranteed.

A major problem is the pitifully small volume supplied in these packages, usually 5 grams, which is nowhere near enough to ensure a successful start to fermentation. 50-100 grams is a more appropriate quantity. Yeast does not like to be mucked about with, and any yeast is going to object to being processed and then thrust into a foil package. Neither is it going to like it much when it is unexpectedly unpackaged and thrust into a home-brew wort. It needs time to adapt to the conditions in which it finds itself. I consider the making of a yeast starter culture essential. The mere sprinkling of a few grains of dried yeast on to your wort is simply asking for trouble.

## Yeast starter culture

The average packaged yeast in Britain contains about 5 grams, nowhere near enough to ensure a rapid start to the fermentation of a 25 litre brew. It is essential that our beer is supplied with an adequate quantity of active yeast to ensure that it is able rapidly to establish itself and form a protective head before bacteria have a chance to gain a foothold. Commercial breweries pitch with about 1½ pounds of yeast per barrel, which equates to about 100 grams per 25 litre home brew batch. Although we do not necessarily require as much as 100 grams, the actual quantity is unimportant, but we do require a lot more than 5 grams if a reliable start is to be achieved.

A yeast starter solution takes only a few minutes to make up. It is made a couple days before we plan to brew and ensures that we have an adequate quantity of active yeast, grown under sterile conditions, before we begin to brew. We can confirm that the yeast is viable, active and bacteriologically sound before committing it to a 25 litre batch. This minimises the risk of later problems with yeast performance or infection. The lag phase, i.e. the time between pitching the yeast and something starting to happen, is reduced considerably because the yeast has converted to aerobic respiration, and is actively multiplying before it is pitched.

It is important to ensure that a yeast starter does not inadvertently become a bacteria starter as well; therefore it is essential that a starter is prepared under conditions of the greatest sterility that we are able to achieve. Unfortunately Pyrex laboratory glassware, autoclaves and Cornelius flasks are not everyday pieces of kitchen equipment. Therefore we must do the best we can with the available equipment.

A combination of chemical sterilisation and heat is the easiest way of ensuring a sterile medium. I use a standard, "dumpy" style, one-pint milk bottle as a culturing flask because it is designed to withstand boiling water and it will accept a winemaker's airlock and rubber bung. The procedure is straightforward enough:

1. Sterilise a standard one-pint milk bottle, an air lock, a rubber bung, and a small funnel using domestic bleach, Chempro SDP or similar. After sterilisation rinse the items very thoroughly. Pre-heat the milk bottle and fill it with boiling water from the kettle and leave it to stand.

2. Bring approximately half a pint of water to the boil in a saucepan and then add four tablespoons (55g) of malt extract. Simmer for about a minute, stirring continuously to avoid burning, and then turn off the heat.

3. Carefully empty the hot water from the milk bottle and then pour in the hot malt extract solution via the funnel. The bottle should be about half full. Loosely cover the mouth of the bottle with a piece of aluminium kitchen foil and stand it in a bowl of cold water until it has cooled to room temperature. The solution will cool faster if the bottle is given a shake from time to time in order to remix the contents.

4. When the solution has cooled, and with the foil still covering the neck of the bottle, give it a vigorous shake to admit oxygen into the solution, taking care not to discharge the contents all over the kitchen.

5. When you are sure that the solution has cooled to room temperature, add your yeast, give the bottle a final vigorous shake, fit the sterilised bung and air lock, and stand the starter in a warmish place of about 20°C. Ensure that the outside of the bottle is clean and free from malt extract solution as this will be a potential bug trap.

Do not brew your main batch of beer until you are sure that the yeast is actively fermenting. This will be indicated by the typical frothy head developing and carbon dioxide bubbles propagating through the airlock. The time taken for the starter to become sufficiently active for pitching is dependent upon yeast viability, initial quantity of yeast, and temperature. Anything from about 10 hours to a couple of days can be experienced. If you intend to brew on a Sunday morning you would probably make your yeast starter on a Friday night; it can be kept under airlock for a couple of days until you are ready to brew. Give the starter a sniff before using it to ensure that it smells okay and is therefore likely to be infection free.

The mouth size of milk bottles seem to vary around the country. Some accept a one-gallon demijohn bung, while others only accept the half-gallon bung which is more difficult to obtain. An alternative is simply to plug the mouth of the bottle with cotton wool. Clean the bottle in Chempro SDP and rinse thoroughly before returning it to your milkman. Dried malt extract is available from your homebrew shop and is more convenient than ordinary malt extract syrup when used for this application. Dried malt extract should be stored very carefully because it will absorb moisture from the atmosphere and set in a hard lump. I store mine within a polythene bag in an airtight sandwich box. If it does set hard, break it up with a hammer or rolling pin. It will still be perfectly okay for yeast starter duties.

### Recovering yeast from a bottled beer

The ability to recover yeast from a bottled beer provides a useful method of obtaining obscure yeasts, or yeasts appropriate to a particular beer. Most British bottled beers are filtered or pasteurised these days which removes or kills the yeast. However, some breweries produce a live, bottle-conditioned beer, and there is an increasing number of imported speciality beers which are unpasteurised. The best known, nationally available, live British beer is Worthington White Shield. English home brewers have traditionally used yeast kidnapped from a Guinness bottle. However, live bottle-conditioned Guinness has disappeared. King and Barnes' Festive and Eldridge Pope's Hardy Country Bitter are now available in bottle-conditioned versions. The procedure for propagating yeast from a bottled beer is quite simple:

1. Stand the donor bottle in a cool place and leave it undisturbed for a day or two to allow the yeast to settle to the bottom.

2. Make up a yeast starter using stages 1 to 4 of the procedure described above.

3. When the starter has cooled to room temperature, *carefully* uncap the donor bottle and decant all but the last half-inch of the contents into a glass, taking care to ensure that any yeast sediment is left behind in the bottle.

4. Give the remaining contents of the donor bottle a good shake in order to dislodge any yeast clinging to the bottom of the bottle. Tip the entire contents, dregs and all, into the yeast starter solution, using the funnel. Shake, fit a sterilised airlock, stand in a warm place etc, as above.

5. Drink contents of glass.

Some commercial beers have a very low residual yeast count and it may take several days for signs of activity to show in the starter medium. Some types of yeast pack firmly down on to the bottom of the bottle. Guinness yeast was one of these, which was why home brewers liked it. With these types of yeasts it may be necessary to pour solution from the starter into the donor bottle, shake and pour back into the starter repeatedly until the yeast has been dislodged.

### Propagating yeast

Many home brewers, when they have found a yeast which suits them, will want to continue to use it. If your favourite yeast happens to be a packaged yeast there is no problem with this, unless the packager changes his source of supply or withdraws the product. If, however, your yeast is from a commercial brewery, or from some other obscure source, you will need to propagate the strain yourself. Many home brewers propagate their own yeast because propagation has the advantage of adapting the yeast to perform well in their particular style of beer. Another advantage is that the yeast supply is of known performance and origin, and free from change imposed by commercial packagers.

Although it is possible to recover yeast from the fermentation vessel and store it in a refrigerator (2-5°C) for up to a week, refrigeration or freezing is not really suitable for long term storage in the domestic environment. By far the easiest and best way of storing yeast is to brew a special strong ale for yeast propagation purposes and bottle it. These bottles are stored away in the back of the garage somewhere and forgotten about, except for special occasions and yeast recovery.

The best type of beer to brew for propagation purposes is a strong, dark, all malt, hoppy brew of OG 1065 or greater; the higher the better. The high alcohol and hop content of such a brew will help to keep the beer sound. Yeast seems to perform better in dark brews, and that is the only reason that I specify a dark beer. I doubt if it matters much in reality. Take extra care over sterilisation and cleanliness for this particular brew. If the beer goes off in storage you cannot re-use the yeast. It is best to brew this particular batch during the winter when it is much less likely to become infected. After the bottles have been filled and capped, wash the outside of them with Chempro SDP or household bleach to remove any traces of spilt beer, which could serve as potential bug traps.

Yeast is recovered from the bottles using the techniques described above. You can, of course, recover yeast from your ordinary bottled beers at intermediate times, but the strong 1065 brew should be regarded as your primary source, and you should never allow yourself to run out of it. Always ensure that the beer is sound by smelling and tasting it before re-propagating the yeast. I regularly re-propagate yeast from bottles three and four years old, and you cannot get much longer-term than that!

### Yeast frets (Cask frets)

When transferring beer into barrels or bottles it is important that precautions are taken to ensure that a minimum of air gets into solution. Not only will dissolved air enable unwanted aerobic bacteria to grow, but if the yeast finds a plentiful supply of air it will revert to aerobic respiration and begin to multiply significantly. Not only will this produce an excessive quantity of yeast in the beer, but when the air is used up the yeast will try to adapt to anaerobic respiration again, but it may find a lack of nutrients on which to work and become stuck in a transitionary phase. Under these conditions the yeast will remain in suspension and could take a long time to clear down properly.

This condition can also be caused by an excessive amount of air in the head space of casks. Ideally a cask should be quite full when it is filled, except, perhaps for a little bit of space to allow for liquid expansion with temperature. Not only does a full cask leave insufficient room for a significant amount of air, but the pressure build-up is more reliable because there is no ullage to compress. The pressure build up in the cask aids the clearing process.

If your cask has a significant amount of empty space, it may be beneficial at the time of filling to add some cane sugar primings to build the pressure up quickly. After a couple of days expel air by releasing the cap slightly and then re-seal. Repeat this a couple of days later, and then leave the ale in peace to mature. If you have a gas injector, it may pay to pressurise the empty space artificially.

I am sure that the bad reputation that homebrew has gained for being yeasty and turbid is, in the most part, due to yeast frets caused by having too much air in solution, or in the head-space of casks and bottles.

**View of the mash tun showing the slotted base**

# 6 Water Treatment

*Chemistry is a great science no-one can doubt, and its advantage in brewing*
*seems quite patent to the ordinary practical brewer; although I must confess I*
*am not so enraptured with the science myself in respect to brewing, inasmuch*
*as I am quite satisfied that with any pure spring water, immaterial whether*
*it is Burton water or from any other part of England, and being supplied*
*with the best materials in Malt, and the best East Kent Hops, for Pale Ale, I*
*should be fully satisfied that I shall not need the aid of a chemist.*
*- James Herbert, The Art of Brewing, 1871*

So, the old water chestnut raises its ugly head again. There has probably
been more controversy raised about this particular subject than about any
other aspect of brewing, and it is probably true to say that chapters on water
treatment are the chapters that most home brewers do not bother to read.
This is not surprising when one observes how some authors have struggled
and fought with the subject, and then very often lost the fight. One well-
known home brewing reference book expends 22 pages on the subject of
water treatment. It contains lots of tables, charts, and graphs, and tons of
text, the results of which are totally incomprehensible to the majority of us –
and possibly to the book's author as well. Yet the same book devotes only
five pages to yeast, which is a much more important subject in my view.

The problem is that the quality of brewing water has achieved an elevat-
ed status by popular demand rather than by scientific implication, and
home-brew authors are expected to expound at great lengths upon the subject, whether or not they believe what they are writing.

Controversy over water has raged since Victorian times, when water
quality was a great social issue. The breweries of the day went to great
lengths to advertise the quality of their water supply, and cashed in on
Victorian health fads by producing mineral waters, soda waters, seltzer
waters, potash waters and the like. The relationship between types of water
and brewing has always been known. William Cobbett condemned hard
water as being unsuitable for brewing when he wrote his essay on home
brewing in 1821! His knowledge of brewing seems to stem from a book on
commercial brewing published some years before that date.

Unsuitable water was often used as an excuse for bad brewing. Water
quality was blamed for every ill and it became the scapegoat of many brewers who were unable to match the quality of Burton Pale Ale and the scientific Burton brewers encouraged this misconception. The brewers of
Burton-upon-Trent, who supposedly had the ideal water supply, blamed
"atmospheric electricity" for their cock-ups!

The truth is that water treatment is neither as complex or as important as
a lot of people seem to think. That is not to say that the subject should be
completely ignored, but it is certainly not worth losing any sleep over. The
great London porter brewers of old did not build their breweries in London
because the water suited them. They built their breweries in London

because that was where the people happened to be. Burton-upon-Trent became a brewing town only because a bunch of Benedictine monks, who knew how to brew, happened to live there. Centuries of experience, helped by the River Trent, the Trent and Mersey Canal, and the Midland railway, did the rest for the great Burton brewers. There are breweries located all over the country that have been making perfectly satisfactory ales for two hundred years or more – long before water treatment was ever thought of. There is no domestic water supply in Britain that will make bad beer!

It is probably true to say that in order to duplicate exactly a particular brewer's beer, you will need to duplicate his water supply, but it is also true that most water supplies around Britain will produce acceptable beers without treatment. However, some minerals present in water supplies are detrimental to beer whereas others are beneficial. Therefore, a certain amount of water treatment is usually advantageous, but it can only be regarded as an improvement. Even so, the improvement may not be apparent to the home brewer.

Only a few of the minerals found in water are important as far as brewing is concerned:

**Calcium bicarbonate** is the principal substance causing temporary hardness in our water supplies and is the one mineral that is undesirable in beer. It reacts adversely with the components of the mash, increasing its pH, which is the opposite effect to that desired under normal circumstances. Fortunately it is relatively easy to remove calcium bicarbonate by boiling the water, whereby it is broken down into carbon dioxide and calcium carbonate (common chalk). The carbon dioxide is given off to the atmosphere and the chalk, being insoluble in water, settles out on the bottom of the boiler. The water should be well aerated before boiling because the liberation of the air during boiling will help to drive off the carbon dioxide evolved during the process and prevent it recombining.

**Calcium sulphate (gypsum)** is the principal substance causing permanent hardness in water. It is a beneficial mineral as far as brewing is concerned, which is fortunate because it is difficult to remove. It reacts with the malt during mashing, causing phosphates to precipitate releasing phosphoric acid, which in turn lowers the Ph of the mash, all of which is highly desirable. However, excessive use of it can leave yeast with a deficiency of phosphate and poor yeast performance will result.

**Magnesium sulphate (Epsom salts)** is found in some water supplies, and is again a beneficial mineral. Yeast requires magnesium sulphate as a co-enzyme, which promotes vigorous yeast activity. It is not required in large amounts, which is again fortunate because of its well-known purgative properties. There is probably sufficient mineral present naturally. For water treatment purposes half a teaspoonful per 25 litre batch is adequate.

**Sodium chloride (common salt)** is another mineral often added to water for brewing purposes. Although yeast requires chloride ions, there are probably sufficient supplied by the ingredients. Therefore the benefit of sodium chloride is mostly flavour-related, for much the same reason that salt is added to vegetables when cooking. It acts as a flavour enhancer, smooths out harsh flavours, and is considered to be particularly beneficial for brown ales and stouts. The quantity employed is a matter of taste, and should not be sufficient to impart a distinct salt taste. Two or three teaspoonfuls per 25 litre batch is probably a good starting point.

### Preliminary water treatment

Put 25 litres of aerated water into your brewing boiler and bring to the boil. When the water comes to the boil, add 12g calcium sulphate (2 heaped teaspoons) and 3g common salt (half teaspoon) then boil vigorously for 15 minutes to half an hour. When the boiling period is complete switch off the heat and wait for the precipitate to settle out. Then add 2g Magnesium Sulphate (half teaspoon).

The magnesium sulphate is added last because it can retard the precipitation of carbonates. It dissolves easily. I often add it after racking the treated water off the precipitated chalk, but sometimes directly to the mash. The common salt is a matter of taste; indeed, many home brewers do not bother with it.

This preliminary water treatment is a good starting point irrespective of the type of beer being brewed, and irrespective of your water supply. It is usually easier to perform the water treatment the evening before you intend to brew.

### Aerating the water.

If your domestic kettle furs up heavily, you live in an area where the water is rich in calcium bicarbonate. Removing this bicarbonate by boiling is more efficiently done if the water contains plenty of dissolved air prior to the boiling operation. As it happens, fresh mains water from your kitchen tap is probably rich in dissolved air, particularly if it is dispensed via one of those nozzles with a piece of gauze or perforated plastic inside, which causes the water to foam. On the other hand, the act of filling your boiler will probably admit plenty of air. If you have any doubts about the matter, any sort of spraying action, or merely sloshing your water from one container to another with plenty of mechanical action will admit copious amounts of air. Of course, if you live in an area where the water is not 'chalky', you need not concern yourself with the matter.

### How will I know if my water treatment is okay?

The primary reason for water treatment is to ensure that the mash conditions are correct. The ideal Ph for the mash is about 5.3, although in general the lower it is the better. If, after a trial brew without water treatment, the Ph of the mash is any higher than about 5.8 it may be desirable to perform some sort of water treatment. The addition of calcium sulphate to the water tends to lower the Ph as does removing the calcium bicarbonate. You will not know if you need to treat the water until you begin to brew with it. So it is really a chicken and egg situation. Indicator papers for measuring Ph are available from home brew shops. I prefer those that are manufactured by Johnsons of Hendon. Low cost electronic Ph meters are available from laboratory equipment suppliers.

I am of the opinion that all water used for brewing should be boiled to drive off any purification chemicals employed by the water company. Boiling the water has also the additional advantage that undesirable calcium bicarbonate is precipitated out. In addition, a high degree of sterility is ensured. The main wort boil will drive off purification chemicals of course, but if fresh tap-water is used to adjust original gravity prior to fermentation, some of these are bound to be re-introduced.

# 7 Home Brewing Equipment

*Surely mistakes such as these never ought be made by such scientific brewers as Burton can boast of, not one of whom but what is perfect in the science of chemistry! There they are stationary, the same old thing as twenty or thirty years ago. They make no progress in reference to brewing, always analysing and experimenting; however, we must look out for some wonderful discovery by Professor Somebody after another half a century I suppose; but the professors are a long time bringing their science to a satisfactory issue as far as brewing is concerned. I am of opinion that brewing at the present time is at its highest pitch, as far as perfection goes.*

*– James Herbert, The Art of Brewing, 1871*

To brew decent quality beer a certain amount of equipment is obviously required. Fortunately most of it is relatively inexpensive and, as this book assumes that the reader has done a certain amount of brewing before, the majority of readers will have accumulated most of it. The most expensive item is a good boiler, but the saving made on brewing 25 litres of home brewed beer, when compared to the price of commercial stuff, will more than adequately cover the cost of a boiler.

This book assumes that the following minimum equipment is available: a brewing boiler, two brewing bins with taps and lids, a hydrometer and trial jar, a thermometer, a large home brewer's sieve, a funnel, syphon tubing, weighing equipment, and at least one barrel. If mashing is to be employed, then a grain bag will be required, or the mash tun described below could be constructed. If bottling is envisaged then a minimum of 40 one-pint bottles, crown caps and a capping tool will be required. Some of the items warrant further discussion:

## Boiler

A boiler is an item of equipment that can be considered essential to a keen home brewer. We need to boil large volumes of wort, sometimes in excess of our final volume of beer if we over-sparge a high gravity beer. Malt extract brewers can get away with boiling a smaller volume, but even so, it is desirable to boil a volume of wort as close to our final volume of beer as possible. Kitchen utensils can be pressed into service, particularly if a large four or five gallon dixie is available, but in general, ordinary kitchen utensils are impractical and a decent electric boiler is almost essential.

There are two types of purpose-built, polypropylene home-brewing boilers available in the shops, the Ritchie Bruheat, and the Thorne Electrim. Unfortunately neither of them is provided with a false bottom for the hops to settle on when the boil is complete. This is not an insurmountable problem because we can either make our own or construct a separate hopback vessel, and use that to strain the hops and trub out of the wort; it is just frustrating that the home-brew industry does not provide the proper thing for us. I have invested in a Burco stainless steel catering boiler and for that I have fabricated a perforated false bottom out of copper sheet.

However, as an alternative to a false bottom, the home brewing industry does supply nylon hop bags for containing the hops during the boil. These eliminate the need for a false bottom but they can restrict the all-important vigour of the boil. Ideally the hops should be allowed to boil freely in the wort. However, the use of a hop bag may be useful to those new to brewing, or those who have neither time nor the facilities to make a false bottom or a hopback. Unlike a grain bag, a hop bag should be made from very coarse mesh, almost like garden strawberry netting.

### Separate hopback

An alternative to using an integral false bottom or hop bag in the boiler is to use a separate external vessel a hopback. The hops can be allowed to boil freely in the wort and then be transfered to the hopback when the boil is complete. The trub and hops can then be filtered from the wort in the separate hopback. The home-made mash tun described later is eminently suited for use as a hopback. Alternatively, a hop bag or grain bag can inserted into a standard, unmodified brewing bin (with tap) and the filtering performed by this.

If a separate vessel is employed as a hopback, the hot wort must be transferred to this vessel, a hazardous process. Unfortunately the taps fitted to boilers are not large enough to allow the spent hops to pass through, and will block if an attempt is made to use them. The easiest method of transferring the hot wort from the boiler to the hopback is to bail most of the wort across using a small saucepan. When the volume in the boiler has been reduced to an easily manageable level, tip the remainder into the hopback – hops and all. Allow half an hour or so for everything to settle, and then run off the clear wort via the tap.

### Mashing equipment

Mashing is the process of infusing the malted barley grain in water at a carefully maintained temperature of about 66°C, which enables the enzymes to convert the starch contained in the malt into fermentable sugars. Commercial breweries mash using a special vessel called a mash tun. This is an unheated, well-insulated vessel which has a perforated false bottom to retain the grain so that the wort can easily be drained from the mash. The vessel relies on good heat insulation to maintain the temperature so a heater is not required. My preferred method of mashing uses a home-made, insulated mash tun which closely imitates a commercial brewery mash tun. It is described next:

### Home-made insulated mash tun

This uses two fermentation buckets, one inserted inside the other. The inside one has holes drilled in the base to make a false bottom for run off and sparging, and the outside bucket has a tap fitted to enable the wort to be run off at will. During mashing the contraption is lagged with insulation to prevent heat loss. The device should be known as a *"Home Brewer's*

*Universal Widget"*, because without the lagging it can also serve as a hop back or a lauter tun.

The two bins should be identical, except that the outer bin should have a tap fitted, and the inner bin should not. The inner bin should be equipped with a close fitting lid. The type of bin employed for this application should be of the highly tapered, bucket-shaped variety, not the tall, narrow type which will not allow the inner bin to be inserted far enough inside the outer one.

The base of the inner bin should be drilled with a matrix of 2mm or 3mm holes spaced obout 15mm apart. The hole size is not critical. My bin has a 280mm (11 inch) base and has about 400 3mm ($\frac{1}{64}$ inch) holes drilled symmetrically around it. The outer bin is unmodified apart from having a tap fitted. The tap should be fitted fairly close to the bottom to minimise the amount of wasted space under the false bottom, but do not fit the tap so low that it prevents the bin being stood on a flat surface! The tun is assembled by pushing the drilled inner bin down into the outer bin as far as it will go. It should rest upon the outer bin tap-fixing nut.

**Insulating the home-made mash tun**
During mashing, the tun is insulated by wrapping strips of plastic covered water tank insulation around the outside of the outer bin. The strips are held in position by stretchy luggage straps in my case, but they could also be held in position by string or adhesive tape. During the mash the lid is fitted to the inner bin and more strips of insulation are laid over the top to reduce the heat loss through the lid. An old blanket could serve as insulation, but it may be less efficient. In addition, the insulating strips can be cleaned by wiping a damp cloth over them, whereas a blanket would need to be washed if it got splashed with wort.

Grain disposal is effected by simply pulling the two bins apart, tipping the grains out, and then washing the contraption down with a garden hose.

**Mashing using a grain-bag and boiler**
If you do not wish to turn your hand to drilling holes in a brewing bin, an alternative is to use a grain bag in conjunction with your boiler. Any home-brew shop will supply you with a fine-mesh grain bag. However, grain bags are messy and difficult to use. In addition, the boiler is occupied with mashing duties when it could be better employed elsewhere; heating sparge liquor for instance. However, many home brewers use the grain bag method, and almost every "masher" learned his craft using one.

**Mashing using a floating mash tun**
Some home brewers mash by floating a small, unmodified fermentation bin in their brewing boiler. No grain bag is employed, but a separate vessel is required to separate the grain from the wort. The separate vessel is very similar to a mash tun, only it is called a lauter tun. The home made mash tun decribed above can serve as a lauter tun.

## Sparging equipment

Sparging entails gently spraying hot water, at a temperature of about 77-80°C, over the goods in the mash tun to rinse out the sugars. Some home brewers simply pour jugfuls of hot water over the surface of the mash, but this can have the disadvantage of breaking up the mash bed. Other home brewers use a small watering can and spray hot water with this. I use a "Haws Genuine" brass watering can rose connected to my boiler by a length of polypropylene pipe.

However, it is not absolutely essential to have special sparging equipment. The instructions for grain brewing in chapter 10 give a simple method of rinsing the sugars from the grains.

## Barrels (casks)

When you have brewed your beer you will obviously need some form of container in which to mature and keep it, and from which to dispense it. There are a number of casks of various shapes and sizes available from home brew shops. I have a preference for the horizontal type of cask supplied by Ritchie Products, for no valid reason other than that it seems to me to be a *sensible* cask. This cask, affectionately known as the piggy, is the same shape as a traditional cask and lies horizontally like a traditional cask. The traditional beer barrel has evolved over a period of a 1000 years or more; the result of the accumulated experience of generations of men. I am not one to let all of that wisdom go to waste.

Unfortunately, most of the casks currently available to us are too big! Ideally the cask should be quite full when an ale is stowed away for maturation. Air is the enemy of sound beer. The best way of keeping air out of contact with the beer is to make sure that there is no room for it! The home-brew casks from the various manufacturers vary in size and the actual volume is often much larger than the quoted volume. The low-cost upright home-brew casks hold about 25 litres (5½ gallons) to the brim, and the otherwise excellent Ritchie horizontal cask holds about 30 litres (6½ gallons) to the brim. To fill a 30 litre cask would need about a 34 litre (7½ gallon) fermentation bin, and about a 36 litre (8 gallon) boiler – much larger than the equipment that is actually available.

A brewer's pin (4½ gallon cask) is a more appropriate cask size. We lose about half a gallon of ale during fermentation and the various syphoning and racking operations, so a pin is ideal for use in conjunction with our five-gallon fermenting bins and other equipment. The pioneering home brewers who founded the hobby used ex-brewery wooden pins which were made redundant during the keg revolution. Take-away polypins can be pressed into service, and have the advantage of being collapsible to exclude air, but they are really designed as a one-trip throw-away container and are far from convenient as far as home brewing is concerned.

I have opted for the convenience of the wide-necked casks available via the home-brew trade, and have accepted the inevitability that a certain amount of air space (ullage) will be present. The effects of this can be minimised by purging some of the air out of this space by carefully vented and re-sealing the cask a couple of days after filling.

When sterilising the barrel caps, separate the sealing ring from the cap to ensure that both cap and ring are properly sterilised. Give the ring a light smear of petroleum jelly (Vaseline) before refitting it, which will help ensure a perfect seal. The threads of the caps should also be given a smear of petroleum jelly. I have some spare caps for my barrels with the safety valves disabled (blocked off) so that I can close a barrel down tightly if need be, for stowing an ale away for a long period, for example. A useful accessory is a cap spanner to help remove difficult caps. These are available from home brewing suppliers.

### Hydrometer

A hydrometer is a useful and inexpensive item of equipment which enables us to measure the specific gravity of our wort at various stages during fermentation. This enables a check to be maintained on how fermentation is progressing. The typical brewer's open type of glass hydrometer which is used in conjunction with a trial jar is the most suitable type for our purposes.

The density of a fluid is temperature dependent and hydrometers are calibrated for use at one particular temperature, usually 20°C. To find the SG of a fluid which is at a different temperature from that for which the hydrometer is calibrated requires the use of a correction table. Hot fluids should be cooled as much as possible before measurement is attempted because greater measurement errors occur at higher temperatures.

Correction table for 20°C hydrometers

| Temperature °C | Correction |
|:---:|:---:|
| 4-10 | -2 |
| 10-18 | -1 |
| 18-22 | 0 |
| 22-26 | +1 |
| 26-29 | +2 |
| 29-32 | +3 |
| 32-35 | +4 |

At a given temperature the correction factor is simply added or subtracted from the indicated gravity reading as appropriated. Example: If a sample of wort has a temperature of 27°C and an indicated gravity of 1045 (1.045), the correction factor is +2, therefore true gravity is 1047.

### Wheeler's widgets

If we British are well-known for our inventive genius, our scientific acumen, and our brilliant application to all things technical; then why is it that our syphon tubes float? The home brewing industry has been established for more than 30 years, and it still supplies us with syphon tubes that float or get dragged out of the wort by their own weight. The glass syphon attachments break as soon as you look at them and the plastic attachments fall apart at critical moments. A task which should be the simplest of all home-brew operations, that of syphoning a fluid from one vessel to another, often turns out to be the most difficult.

The solution to this problem is to obtain a couple of 11 inch (280mm) lengths of stainless steel motor vehicle brake piping, or small-bore copper tubing, and insert these into the ends of the syphon tube. The brake pipe should be very slightly larger than the inside diameter of the syphon tubing. The plastic syphon tubing is softened by dunking it in hot water, and it is then forced onto the end of the brake pipe. Hey presto! You have a syphon tube that stays under the surface of the beer.

These extensions also make bottle filling a two-handed rather than three-handed operation and reduce the possibility of excessive aeration. It is easy to thrust the pipe to the bottom of the bottle while controlling the flow by squeezing the syphon tubing. Aeration is eliminated and sound beer is assured.

A large old-fashioned bulldog clip, available from stationers, will clamp syphon tubing to the edge of your fermentation bin, and save it from regularly being dragged out of the bin by its own weight. Pet shops sell widgets, intended for fish tank aerators, which will clamp on to your syphon tubing and enable you to adjust the flow should you wish to do so.

## Cleaning and sterilisation

Needless to say, everything that comes into contact with the beer should be thoroughly cleaned and sterilised immediately before use. Apart from the obvious things like bins, lids, barrels, and bottles, the smaller items such as hydrometers, thermometers, funnels, paddles and spoons should also be sterilised. The taps on barrels and bins should be frequently removed and soaked in sterilising solution, as should the caps of barrels. Special attention should be paid to syphon tubing; it is particularly difficult to clean. It should be thoroughly cleaned and sterilised both inside and out.

Domestic bleach is a powerful cleaner and steriliser, and it has served home brewers well for many years. A tablespoon per gallon of water is more than adequate to ensure sterilisation, making it cheap and effective. The items should be thoroughly rinsed afterwards. Proprietary cleaner/sterilisers such as Chempro SDP are available. They are inexpensive and are designed for the job.

Probably the most tedious task in home brewing is the cleaning and ster-ilisation of all the bits and bobs required for a brewing session. I often dis-tribute this tedium by sterilising the equipment that I am going to need the day before I brew. Cleaned and sterilised lids are fitted to clean and ster-ilised bins after placing all the bits and bobs such as thermometers, hydrometers, trial jars, paddles, and spoons inside the bins. The items will remain clean within this sealed environment for a day or two.

# 8 Brewing Instructions – Method A

## Easy Brewing Method – Malt Extract – No Mash Required

Those recipes that only use the ingredients pale malt, crystal malt, black malt, roast barley, or sugars and syrups, are suitable for brewing using this simple brewing method. With this method no mash is required; the pale malt is replaced by malt extract and all the ingredients are simply boiled together in the boiler. Any type of malt extract can be used, but an ordinary, non-diastatic extract is preferred.

It should be appreciated that not all recipes are suitable for brewing by this method. Those recipes that require ingredients other than the above-mentioned cannot be brewed by this way. A selection of recipes that are suitable are indicated in the beers index by an asterisk (*). The recipes thus marked will specify in a footnote to the main recipe the quantity of malt extract to be used.

## Preparation

Choose a recipe indicated with a (*) in the beers index. Simply omit any pale malt, mild ale malt, or amber malt called for in the recipe and replace it with the quantity of light coloured malt extract specified in the footnote to the recipe. Ordinary malt extract can be used, the special diastatic type is not necessary.

Make up a yeast starter solution a couple of days before you intend to brew.

Stand the container of malt extract in hot water for five or ten minutes prior to brewing in order to soften it.

## The boil

Put about 18 litres (4 gallons) of water into the boiler and heat to about 40°C. Stir in the malt extract and other grains, but not the sugars or hops, and then bring to the boil. Add the first batch of hops as soon the wort comes to the boil, and add any sugars or syrups called for about halfway through. A good, vigorous boil for a period of about one-and-a-half to two hours is required.

About 15 minutes before the end of the boiling period, the second batch of hops and the Irish moss (if used) are added. Irish moss helps to precipitate haze-forming proteins out of the wort, but there is little benefit to be gained from using it in conjunction with dark beers. When the wort has been boiled for the desired length of time the boiler is switched off and a period is allowed for the trub and hop debris to settle.

If you have a perforated false bottom fitted to your boiler, or if you are using a hop bag, the wort can be run into a collection vessel, care being taken to ensure that as much debris as possible is left behind in the boiler, filtered by the bed of hops. If you do not have either of these devices then the contents of the boiler should be tipped carefully into a separate hopback and the filtering effected there. If the first runnings are turbid they should be returned to the hopback for re-filtering.

**Wort cooling**

The process from here onwards is identical to the full mash process (method C). Continue from the sub-heading Wort Cooling on page 45 and help save half a rain forest.

**The boiler showing the false bottom where hops settle**

# 9 Brewing Instructions – Method B

## Intermediate Brewing – Malt Extract Mash – No Mash Tun Required

Those recipes that are not suitable for brewing using Brewing Method A described in the previous section, can be brewed using this slightly more complicated method. No mash tun is required; all the work is done in the boiler.

The pale malt is simply replaced by *diastatic* malt extract, and a simple mash is developed by holding the temperature of the boiler at about 66°C for about 30 minutes before boiling. A special type of malt extract known as diastatic malt extract is required for these recipes. Diastatic malt extract contains the enzymes necessary to convert the starch contained in cereal adjuncts into sugars; the best known is EDME DMS.

A selection of suitable recipes is indicated in the beers index by a minus sign (-). The recipes thus marked will specify in a footnote to the main recipe the quantity of malt extract to be used.

### Preparation

Choose a recipe indicated with a (-) in the beers index. Simply omit any pale malt, mild ale malt, or amber malt called for in the recipe and replace it with the quantity of light coloured diastatic malt extract specified in the footnote to the recipe. It is important that diastatic malt extract is used. EDME DMS (Diastatic Malt Syrup) is available from specialist home brew shops. You are unlikely to find it in other outlets such as Boots the chemist. Make up a yeast starter solution a couple of days before you intend to brew. Stand the container of malt extract in hot water for five or ten minutes prior to brewing in order to soften the contents.

### The malt extract mash (partial mash)

Put about 18 litres (4 gallons) of water into the boiler and heat to about 40°C. Stir in the malt extract and other grains, but not sugars or hops. Very slowly raise the temperature to 66°C and hold there for about 30 minutes. Monitor carefully and try to maintain 66°C for this standing period. It doesn't matter if the temperature fluctuates somewhat, but take great pains to ensure that the temperature does not exceed 70°C. Cold water can be added to lower the temperature in an emergency.

### The boil

When the 30 minute standing period has elapsed, top up the boiler with more water if necessary, then slowly raise the temperature to about 75°C, and then to boiling point as fast as you wish. Add the first batch of hops as soon the wort comes to the boil, and add any sugars or syrups called for about halfway through. A good, vigorous boil for a period of about 1½ to 2 hours is required.

About 15 minutes before the end of the boiling period, the second batch of hops and the Irish moss (if used) are added. Irish moss helps to precipitate haze-forming proteins out of the wort, but there is little benefit to be gained from using it in conjunction with dark beers. When the wort has been boiled for the desired length of time the boiler is switched off and a period is allowed for the trub and hop debris to settle.

If you have a perforated false bottom fitted to your boiler, or if you are using a hop bag, the wort can be run into a collection vessel, care being taken to ensure that as much debris as possible is left behind in the boiler, filtered by the bed of hops. If you are not using either of these devices then the contents of the boiler should be carefully tipped into a separate hopback and the filtering effected there. If the first runnings are turbid they should be returned to the hopback for re-filtering.

**Wort cooling**

The process from here onwards is identical to the full mash process (method C). Go directly to the sub-heading Wort Cooling on page 45.

# 10 Brewing Instructions – Method C

## Advanced Brewing – Grain Brewing – Full Mash

All of the recipes in this book are primarily designed for brewing from grain using a full mash. Full mashing is the only brewing method capable of producing exhibition-quality beers, and is the only way of getting close to emulating the commercial beer recipes revealed within these pages.

## Preparation

Make up a yeast starter solution a couple of days before you intend to brew. If you treat your water, perform the water treatment the evening before you intend to brew and store it in your barrel. This will save about an hour during the brewing session.

All of the malted grains used in the making of ale need to be crushed before they can be successfully mashed. Crushing the malt is a difficult process to perform without the proper equipment. Home-brew shops can supply the stuff already crushed and it should be purchased in this form. Cereal adjuncts such as flaked maize and torrefied barley do not need to be crushed.

## Mash liquor

Put 25 litres of treated water into the brewing boiler and heat it to about 77°C. When the liquor is up to temperature run the specified volume of mash liquor into the mash tun. Put the lid on the mash tun and wait a few minutes for the temperature to stabilise. After a few minutes have elapsed check that the temperature of the mash liquor is at strike heat (about 72°C). Adjust the temperature if necessary by adding boiling or cold water.

## The mash

When you have assured yourself that the temperature of the mash liquor (water) is at strike heat carefully add the grist and stir it into the liquor to form a thick porridge-like mass. This should be done thoroughly to ensure that there are no dry pockets remaining, else an inefficient mash will result.

The act of adding the cold grain to the hot liquor should lower the temperature of the mass to around 67°C; close to the correct mashing temperature. If the mash is not at the proper temperature quickly adjust it to its correct value by adding boiling or cold water and stirring it well into the mash.

The temperature of the mash should be maintained between the limits of 62°C and 69°C for a period of 1½ hours. Fit the lid, cover it with some insulation, and leave it to stand for the appropriate mashing period. Monitor the temperature periodically and if the temperature falls too low correct it by adding boiling water and stirring it well in. This should not be necessary if the mash tun is properly insulated.

While the mash is in progress ensure that there is sufficient water in the boiler for sparging, and set the boiler to maintain the sparge liquor at a temperature of 77-80°C.

## Running-off

After the mash has stood for the specified length of time, usually about 1½ hours, carefully open the tap on the mash tun and allow the sweet wort to run **slowly** into a collection vessel. Take care to ensure that the flow is not so fast that the grain beds down hard and blocks. The flow should be very low indeed. The grain should act as a filter bed and filter the wort bright. The first runnings may be turbid, and these should be returned carefully to the mash tun until it runs bright.

## Sparging

When the mash tun has been run off, sparging must begin. This means rinsing the grains with hot water maintained at a temperature of 77-80°C. This rinses out the sugars which are trapped in the grains.

Ideally, the sparge should be a light spray, care being taken to ensure that the mash bed does not crack. Sparging should be performed *slowly and carefully!* Monitor the gravity of the spargings and stop sparging when this falls to below about 1005 or when sufficient wort has been collected.

A common sparging technique, known as fly mashing, does not drain the mash bed completely, but supplies sufficient sparge liquor to balance the outflow from the mash tun and keep the mash bed floating. This technique is probably better if a set mash is likely, but may not be as efficient as sparging.

A simple method of rinsing, which does not require additional equipment, is re-mashing, which is what the brewers of old did. When the first runnings from the mash have drained, the tap is closed and the mash tun is gently re-charged with water at about 80°C. It is then stirred thoroughly and left to stand for about 15 minutes. After the standing period the mash tun is run off as before. This operation is repeated until the collection vessel is full, or the gravity is below 1005.

## The boil

Once the wort has been collected the boiler should be topped up with water to a volume as near to the final volume as can be achieved, remembering to leave sufficient headroom to accommodate the foam produced during boiling. The boil is then begun.

Add the first batch of hops as soon the wort comes to the boil, and add any sugars or syrups called for about halfway through. A good, vigorous boil for a period of about 1½ to 2 hours is required.

About 15 minutes before the end of the boiling period, the second batch of hops and the Irish moss (if used) are added. Irish moss helps to precipitate haze-forming proteins out of the wort, but there is little benefit to be gained from using it in conjunction with dark beers. When the wort has been boiled for the desired length of time the boiler is switched off and a period is allowed for the trub and hop debris to settle.

If you have a perforated false bottom fitted to your boiler, or if you are using a hop bag, the wort can be run directly into a collection vessel, care being taken to ensure that as much debris as possible is left behind in the boiler, filtered by the bed of hops. If you are not using either of these devices then the contents of the boiler should be tipped carefully, or bailed into a separate hopback and the filtering effected there. If the first runnings are turbid they should be returned to the hopback for re-filtering.

## Wort cooling

The next important stage is wort cooling. The wort must be cooled to about 25°C before it is safe to pitch the yeast. If you are spreading your brewing activity over two days there is probably no harm in fitting a sterilised lid to the bin and allowing the wort to cool naturally, overnight perhaps.

However, it could take many hours for the wort to cool down naturally to a temperature at which it is safe to pitch the yeast. Forced cooling allows us to get on with the job more quickly and reduces the possibility of infection by bacteria.

Although some home brewers have made a simple cooling apparatus by using submerged copper piping, through which cold water is passed, by far the most common method employed is to stand the bin containing the hot wort in a slightly larger vessel containing cold water. As long as the hot wort is stirred regularly to equalise the temperature, and the cold water is changed as it heats up, cooling is effected quite quickly. The kitchen sink, an old tin bath, a redundant dustbin, or if you want to take risks, the domestic bath, can be employed. As long as the wort is regularly stirred, the cooling water does not need to come very far up the side of the bin.

## Wort aeration

After cooling, the wort is adjusted to the correct specific gravity by adding cold water, and then it is aerated.

Yeast needs a certain amount of dissolved air to be present in the wort at the start of fermentation in order to multiply and establish itself. The wort boil drives off all the air, so it is important to put some back. This can be achieved by pouring the wort vigorously from one bin to another, generating lots of swirling motion and plenty of mechanical action. Alternatively simply running the wort slowly from one bin to another via the tap is all that is required. In this case just one transfer would be sufficient. The wort should be cool before this action is performed because the solubility of oxygen is greater at low temperatures.

# Fermentation

Ensure that the temperature of the wort is below 30°C before the yeast starter is pitched. The contents of the yeast starter bottle are added to the wort and fermentation will begin. After pitching stand the fermentation vessel in a convenient place where the temperature can be maintained between about 18°C and 22°C, optimum about 20°C. The lid can be fitted to the bin until the yeast head is beginning to form, but should be removed afterwards.

When the head has established itself the surface will contain some dark floccules and trub brought up with the yeast. These should be skimmed off, taking care to cause the minimum of disturbance to the rest of the head.

## Yeast skimming

Many home brewing books recommend frequent yeast skimming. I do not go along with this. I do not believe in continually interfering with the ale. The only time that I physically skim yeast is if it is in danger of spilling over the sides of the bin, or if undesirable things are on the surface of it as mentioned in the previous paragraph, or if it is in danger of collapsing into the ale at the end of fermentation. While the yeast is sitting on top of the ale it is protecting it from airborne bacteria, and that is why open-fermented ales use top-working yeasts.

I use the dropping system, which is the method that all the famous pale ale breweries practised, and some breweries still do, Morlands of Abingdon being one of them. This entails simply transferring the ale to another vessel about half way through fermentation, leaving any undesirable matter behind.

## Dropping

After the ale has been fermenting for a couple of days, when it has attenuated to about half of the original gravity, the fermenting wort should be carefully transferred into another clean and sterilised fermentation vessel and fermentation completed in this. The beer should be syphoned from one container to another, taking care to leave as much yeast and sediment as possible behind in the primary vessel and taking care to admit the minimum of air into solution; although some air may be beneficial for certain strains of yeast. This can be achieved by using a syphon tube, the outlet of which should always be kept submerged under the transferred beer.

This process removes the beer from the sediment that has accumulated on the bottom of the primary vessel. This sediment contains trub, dead yeast cells and other unwanted matter. The dirty primary yeast head is also left behind. A new protective head will soon form on the surface of the transferred beer. The lid can be loosely laid on the bin until the new head has formed. The quality of the ale is much improved by dropping.

## Barrelling

When fermentation has stopped, or when the specific gravity has fallen close to final gravity, it is time for barrelling. I often transfer my ale to an intermediate vessel first, fit the lid and leave it to stand in a cool place for about 12 hours in an attempt to encourage more yeast to settle out; but it is not an essential stage and many home brewers do not bother.

Transfer of the beer from fermentation vessel to barrel should be effected by means of a syphon tube. Care must be taken to allow a minimum amount of air to come into contact with the beer by ensuring that the outlet end of the tube always remains submerged under the beer being transferred. Take care not to transfer any sediment. Ideally the barrels should be filled quite full, but that is difficult to achieve with the equipment currently available to us. The barrel should then be stowed away and the ale matured for an appropriate period.

If your barrel has a large amount of air space remaining, the air should be expelled by carefully releasing and re-sealing the barrel cap after two or three days, and it may be beneficial to add about 50 grams of cane sugar primings at the time of filling to generate conditioning gas rapidly.

## Maturation

The stronger the beer, the longer the maturation period should be. Weak beers require a minimum of about three weeks, strong beers, a month or two. All beers benefit from an extended period of maturation. The weakest beers will keep for at least three months and the strongest several years.

## Bottling

All beer destined for bottling should first be matured for a time in the barrel. Bottling straight from the fermentation vessel is bad practice and should be avoided. A bottle is a tightly sealed container, and the volatile fusel oil products of fermentation have no way of escape. Even the worst commercial breweries mature their bottled beers in a conditioning tank before bottling. Weak beers will need a week or two in barrel, strong beers longer still – perhaps a month, and very strong beers for as long as your patience lasts. The ideal time to bottle is just after the ale has cleared in barrel.

The barrel should be vented by releasing the cap slightly a day or so before bottling is to begin and the beer should have dropped bright before bottling is attempted. The bottles should be filled by means of a syphon tube that reaches to the bottom of the bottle, and the normal precautions should be taken to ensure that a minimum of air is absorbed. They should be filled leaving about half an inch of space in the neck, and the crown caps should be sterilised in Chempro SDP or boiling water before use. The bottles should be stored for a minimum of a month, preferably longer.

You would not go far wrong by following Bass's instructions of 1880:

# BASS'S BOTTLING INSTRUCTIONS (1880)

1. Ale should not be bottled during summer, or in warm weather. Home bottling should be completed by the end of June at the latest. Summer-brewed ale should, however, be bottled as soon as it gets into condition.

2. When ale is received, it should be at once placed, bung upwards on the scantling in the cellar, so as to allow the porous spiles to work; when thus placed it must be left undisturbed.

3. Each cask is usually provided with one or more porous pegs in the bung, which will carry off the gas generated by fermentation. It will only be necessary to make any alteration with regard to these pegs in the case of their having become so much clogged that the cask would burst if the requisite vent were not given; or in the opposite case of a tendency in the beer to become flat, when hard spiles must be substituted.

4. The cellar ought to be WELL-VENTILATED, kept perfectly clean, and as cool as possible. Underground cellars are usually the best.

5. Immediately the beer is bright and sparkling, and in a quiet state, not fermenting, it is in the proper condition to be bottled.

6. If from any cause the ale should not become fit for bottling in the usual time, it will generally be sufficient to pass it through the grounds again, i.e, roll it over and put it up again on the scantling.

7. Ordinary bottling taps, with long tubes reaching almost to the bottom of the bottles, are recommended. All taps, pipes, and vessels used for ale should be kept scrupulously clean.

8. The bottles when filled should be corked without delay.

9. The bottles should be piled standing upright. Should the ale be sluggish in ripening, the bottles may be laid down; but this is seldom necessary.

10. Bottled ale is never fit to be sent out under a month. It takes at least that time to acquire the bottled flavour.

11. As the ale ripens in bottle a sediment is thrown down. In uncorking a bottle, therefore, be very careful to avoid disturbing this.

12. In decanting, pour out the ale in a jug, carefully keeping back the sediment within the bottle.

NB: With respect to ale consumed on draught, remarks Nos. 2 to 6 inclusive are equally applicable, always taking care to give as little vent as possible.

## Fining and priming

Fining is the addition of a clearing agent, either gelatine or isinglass, which assists in clearing the beer by dragging yeast out of suspension.

Priming is the practice of adding fermentable sugars to the cask in order to bring the beer rapidly into condition, that is, to make the beer lively, by encouraging a secondary fermentation which puts carbon dioxide gas into solution.

A well-brewed beer, kept its proper time, should not need priming or fining. A good yeast will clear down unaided, and residual dextrins contained in the beer will slowly ferment and produce perfect condition.

A home brewer may need recourse to fining or priming under certain circumstances. A beer may not be clearing well and fining may be required to help it along. A beer that uses a high proportion of cane sugar in its makeup may be deficient in slowly-fermenting dextrins so may need priming to help it get into condition. Also, a home brewer may want to prime and fine for the same reason that a commercial brewery does; to get a beer into drinkable condition in the shortest possible time. It should not be necessary to prime and fine bottled beers.

Proper liquid isinglass finings can be purchased from a home-brew shop, and should be used as directed on the bottle. The finings should always be mixed with a small quantity of beer before adding them to the cask. Isinglass should always be stored in a cool place, preferably the refrigerator.

An alternative to isinglass is ordinary Davis Gelatine, obtainable from supermarkets. One 12-gram satchet is dissolved in a cupful of hot water as directed on the packet, allowed to cool, then mixed with a little beer before adding it to the cask. Keep the solution covered with a saucer while it is cooling.

White or dark cane sugar can be used for priming if the beer is to be drunk within a short period of time. Malt extract or maize-derived glucose syrup may be better if the beer is to be kept longer. In each case 50-100 grams, made into a syrup with about 250 millilitres of boiling water, will do the trick. Allow the solution to cool, and keep it covered while it is doing so.

Finings should not be added until the beer has had some time to mature, at least a week should have elapsed after barrelling, preferably three weeks. Finings will not work properly if the yeast is still active and not ready to drop. In any case, there is no point in fining until a few days before the beer is to be drunk. Isinglass finings will fine a beer within about twelve hours of being added.

# 11 Mild Ale Recipes

*If statistics could be obtained as to the quantity of beer spoiled by the scientific brewer, and also by the ordinary practical man, I am confident that it will be favourable to the latter, for I believe that there have been more ales spoiled from experimenting, and scientific men brewing from their theoretical knowledge, than from any other cause.*

*James Herbert The Art of Brewing, 1871*

A good, well-brewed mild ale is a superb drink and was England's most popular beer, particularly among working people, until just after the Second World War. Its popularity waned from then on, partly because the brewers insisted on progressively weakening the product or faking it by merely adding caramel to their running light ales, and partly because a "cloth cap" stigma became attached to the drinking of dark beers.

There is no doubt that many brewers attempted to palm off their drinkers with inferior imitation products; the drinkers responded by rejecting mild and moving to other beers. I feel that cask mild ale would still be on every pub counter had the brewers (and publicans) supplied quality products. The brewers' argument was that the mild ale market was price driven, and that people would only drink it if it was cheap.

I feel that this is clearly a case of the brewers shooting themselves in the foot. The truth of the matter is that a true-to-type, high quality, dark mild ale needs to be brewed as a separate gyle, i.e. specially brewed as a mild ale, and this did not fit in with the brewers' mega-brewing, parti-gyle mentality of the time. It was far easier to fake the stuff by adding caramel to a parti-gyled standard beer. Many commercial mild ales are fakes, but there are still a few genuine ones about, particularly in the Midlands.

The term *mild* means "not bitter" and has nothing at all to do with strength. In the modern sense it means "mildly hopped", although in the old sense it meant not sour!

The origins of the term mild ale stem from the early days of commercial brewing. In those days many people did not feel that a beer had matured properly until it was beginning to turn sour, i.e. until an acetic acid taste was beginning to develop. However, the degree of acidity was a matter of individual taste and differences in personal preference were overcome by publicans supplying two grades of beer: Mild beer, which was a fresh immature beer; and Stale beer which was the same stuff only it had been kept for up to a year and was beginning to turn sour. The customer mixed these in his tankard in appropriate quantities to give him the desired tang. Some moneyed people made a trade of buying mild and keeping it until it was sour and selling it to the publicans at a profit. Stale was therefore more expensive than mild so many people drank mild on its own and this eventually came to dominate public taste, particularly outside of London where a taste for an acetic tang did not seem to develop to the same degree.

The milds of say 300 years ago were simply immature versions of the standard brown beers of the day, which were brewed using the only malt widely available: brown malt. Brown malt was kilned over a hardwood fire which smoked the malt as it dried it, giving it a rich smoky character. Smoked malt was considered essential to a beer, as peat-smoked malt is considered essential to whisky today.

Over the centuries dark mild has evolved into its present form, after being firstly influenced by eighteenth century Porter, nineteenth century tastes, and then twentieth century greed, the term "mild" coming to mean lightly hopped rather than not sour. The character of a modern dark mild is derived from the use of dark roasted malts and cereal adjuncts, giving it a luscious depth of flavour. In 1805 a mild would have had a gravity of OG 1085. In 1871 mild was typically brewed at OG 1070 and in 1913 at OG 1050. Alas, a modern-day mild would be about OG 1034 – twentieth century greed.

Light coloured mild ales are "mild" in the literal sense, i.e. they are an ordinary pale ale which is mildly hopped. They are not expected to have the same depth of character as genuine dark mild ales. Years ago many breweries produced a light-coloured mild ale called "AK", but they have all forgotten why they termed it such, and there is some debate as to the origin of the term. James Herbert in "The Art of Brewing", 1871, had this to say:

*AK ALE; This class of ales has very much come into use, mostly for private families, it being a light tonic Ale, and sent out by most brewers at one shilling per gallon. The gravity of this Ale is usually brewed at 20lbs [OG 1056].*

At OG 1056, AK was quite a lot weaker than the dark mild ales of the time, which, according to the same author, were brewed at 25lbs (OG 1070). The term AK is probably derived from "Amber Kitchen Ale", being a cheaper quality of ale that you would supply for the refreshment of your servants, as was customary at one time.

Amber ales, dinner ales, kitchen ales, mild ales, and table beers figure strongly in nineteenth century brewery price lists, sometimes all at once. A remote possibility is that AK began as a blend of amber ale and keeping ale (stock ale), at a time when the blending of different ales was all part of the brewers art. McMullens still brew a light mild they refer to as AK, though it isn't brewed at OG 1056!

# Arkell's MASH TUN MILD

A strong dark mild, lightly hopped, an occasional brew from Arkell's Swindon Brewery. Full flavours of malt in the mouth, dry but creamy finish with fine nut character.

Classification:  English Cask-Conditioned Mild Ale

Original gravity:  1040

*In the mash tun*

| | | |
|---|---|---|
| Pale malt: | 3,000 g | (66%) |
| Crystal malt: | 1,400 g | (30%) |

*In the copper*

| | | |
|---|---|---|
| Cane sugar: | 180 g | (4%) |
| Fuggles hops: | 60 g | (start of boil) |

*Typical characteristics*

| | | | |
|---|---|---|---|
| Brewing method: | C; Single infusion mash, top fermented. | | |
| Mash liquor: | 11 litres | Alcohol content: | 4.3 % |
| Mash temperature: | 63°C | Final gravity: | 1009 |
| Mash time: | 90 minutes | Bitterness: | 21 EBU |
| Boil time: | 90 minutes | Final volume: | 23 litres |

MALT EXTRACT VERSION – No mash required

Replace the pale malt with 2,200 grams of non-diastatic, dark-coloured malt extract and brew using Malt Extract Brewing – Method A.

# Bateman's DARK MILD

A fine example of a tasty, dark red mild from Bateman's Wainfleet brewery. Pleasing chewy malt in the mouth, dry finish with roast malt and caramel notes.

Classification:    English Cask-Conditioned Mild Ale

Original gravity:            1033

*In the mash tun*

| | | |
|---|---|---|
| Pale malt: | 2,100g | (60%) |
| Crystal malt: | 420 g | (12%) |
| Chocolate malt: | 175 g | (5% see notes) |
| Torrified wheat: | 140 g | (4%) |

*In the copper*

| | | |
|---|---|---|
| Invert sugar: | 700 g | (19%) |
| Golding hops: | 55 g | (start of boil) |
| Golding hops: | 10 g | (last 15 minutes) |

*Typical characteristics*

| | | | |
|---|---|---|---|
| Brewing method: | C; Single infusion mash, top fermented. | | |
| Mash liquor: | 9 litres | Alcohol content: | 3.8 % |
| Mash temperature: | 63°C | Final gravity: | 1005 |
| Mash time: | 90 minutes | Bitterness: | 22 EBU |
| Boil time: | 90 minutes | Final volume: | 23 litres |

NOTES

Bateman's actually use brewer's caramel for colouring. The 5% chocolate malt has been added to this particular recipe for colour.

MALT EXTRACT VERSION – Partial mash required

Replace the pale malt with 1,500 grams of diastatic malt extract such as EDME DMS. Brew using Malt Extract Brewing – Method B.

# Boddington's MILD

Pleasant, easy-drinking tawny mild ale from Boddington's Strangeways brewery in Manchester. The complex combination of hops is typical of Boddington's beers.

Classification:   English Cask-Conditioned Mild Ale

Original gravity:          1032

*In the mash tun*

| | | |
|---|---|---|
| Pale malt: | 3,000 g | (85%) |
| Crystal malt: | 325 g | (9%) |
| Chocolate malt: | 70 g | (2%) |

*In the copper*

| | | |
|---|---|---|
| Invert sugar: | 145 g | (4%) |
| Fuggles hops: | 20 g | (start of boil) |
| Goldings hops: | 15 g | (start of boil) |
| Whitbread Goldings: | 10 g | (start of boil) |
| Bramling Cross hops: | 5 g | (start of boil) |
| Northdown hops: | 5 g | (start of boil) |

*Typical characteristics*

| | | | |
|---|---|---|---|
| Brewing method: | C; Single infusion mash, top fermented. | | |
| Mash liquor: | 8 litres | Alcohol content: | 3.4% |
| Mash temperature: | 63°C | Final gravity: | 1007 |
| Mash time: | 90 minutes | Bitterness: | 22 EBU |
| Boil time: | 90 minutes | Final volume: | 23 litres |

NOTES

Boddington's OB MILD (overleaf) is a simpler version of the same beer. Boddington add some caramel to their milds for colouring, and they prime with cane sugar.

# Boddington's OB MILD

Darkish mild from Boddington's Strangeways brewery, Manchester. Hard to distinguish from its 'Mild' stablemate in the previous recipe. Malt and chocolate flavours in the mouth, light hop and nut finish.

Classification:     English Cask-Conditioned Mild Ale

Original gravity:          1032

*In the mash tun*

| | | |
|---|---|---|
| Pale malt: | 3,000 g | (85%) |
| Crystal malt: | 325 g | (9%) |
| Chocolate malt: | 70 g | (2%) |

*In the copper*

| | | |
|---|---|---|
| Invert cane sugar: | 145 g | (4%) |
| Fuggles hops: | 25 g | (start of boil) |
| Goldings hops: | 20 g | (start of boil) |
| British Columbian hops: | 8g | (start of boil) |
| Fuggles hops: | 10 g | (last 15 minutes) |
| Irish moss: | 1 tsp | (last 15 minutes) |

*Typical characteristics*

| | | | |
|---|---|---|---|
| Brewing method: | C; Single infusion mash, top fermented. | | |
| Mash liquor: | 8 litres | Alcohol content: | 3.4% |
| Mash temperature: | 63°C | Final gravity: | 1007 |
| Mash time: | 90 minutes | Bitterness: | 22 EBU |
| Boil time: | 90 minutes | Final volume: | 23 litres |

## NOTES

British Columbian hops can be omitted or substituted by Goldings if difficulty is encountered in obtaining them. Boddington add some caramel to their milds for colouring, and they prime with cane sugar.

# Burtonwood DARK MILD

Fine example of a characterful dark mild from Burtonwood Brewery in Warrington, Cheshire. Rich, nutty malt in the mouth, good hop finish with a hint of chocolate.

Classification:    English Cask-Conditioned Mild Ale

Original gravity:          1032

*In the mash tun*

| | | |
|---|---|---|
| Mild ale malt: | 2,500 g | (70%) |
| Crystal malt: | 250 g | (7%) |
| Black malt: | 140 g | (4%) |
| Torrefied wheat: | 320 g | (9%) |

*In the copper*

| | | |
|---|---|---|
| Invert cane sugar: | 350 g | (10%) |
| Challenger hops: | 7 g | (start of boil) |
| Progress hops: | 9 g | (start of boil) |
| Whitbread Goldings: | 13 g | (start of boil) |
| Fuggles hops: | 18 g | (start of boil) |
| Fuggles hops: | 5 g | (last 15 minutes) |

*Typical characteristics*

| | | | |
|---|---|---|---|
| Brewing method: | C; Single infusion mash, top fermented. | | |
| Mash liquor: | 8 litres | Alcohol content: | 3.4% |
| Mash temperature: | 63°C | Final gravity: | 1007 |
| Mash time: | 90 minutes | Bitterness: | 22 EBU |
| Boil time: | 90 minutes | Final volume: | 23 litres |

NOTES

Burtonwood Brewery add about 2 per cent caramel for additional colour in their mild ale. The black malt has been increased in this version to compensate.

# Chester's BEST MILD

A dark, malty mild from Chester's brewery in Sheffield, a subsidiary of Whitbread. Thin, slightly astringent, with a dry finish and chocolate notes.

Classification:    English Cask-Conditioned Mild Ale

Original gravity:            1032

*In the mash tun*

| | | |
|---|---|---|
| Pale malt: | 2,500 g | (70%) |
| Chocolate malt: | 175 g | (5%) |
| Torrefied wheat: | 530 g | (15%) |

*In the copper*

| | | |
|---|---|---|
| Invert cane sugar: | 350 g | (10%) |
| Target hops: | 26 g | (start of boil) |

*Typical characteristics*

| | | | |
|---|---|---|---|
| Brewing method: | C; Single infusion mash, top fermented. | | |
| Mash liquor: | 8 litres | Alcohol content: | 3.5% |
| Mash temperature: | 63°C | Final gravity: | 1006 |
| Mash time: | 90 minutes | Bitterness: | 23 EBU |
| Boil time: | 90 minutes | Final volume: | 23 litres |

## NOTES

Chester's add their hops in the form of extracts and pellets, in the ratio 25 per cent Target hop pellets to 75 per cent hop extract.

MALT EXTRACT VERSION – Partial mash required

Replace the pale malt with 1,850 grams of diastatic malt extract such as EDME DMS. Brew using Malt Extract Brewing – Method B.

# Everard's MILD

Pleasant, mellow, mahogany-coloured mild ale from Everard's Brewery in Leicester. Malt in the mouth with some fruit notes.

Classification:   English Cask-Conditioned Mild Ale

Original gravity:        1033

*In the mash tun*

| | | |
|---|---|---|
| Pale malt: | 3,000 g | (78%) |
| Crystal malt: | 450 g | (12%) |
| Flaked maize: | 300 g | ( 8%) |
| Black malt: | 75 g | ( 2%) |

*In the copper*

| | | |
|---|---|---|
| Fuggles hops: | 31 g | (start of boil) |
| Challenger hops: | 19 g | (start of boil) |
| Goldings hops: | 15 g | (last 15 minutes) |

*Typical characteristics*

| | | | |
|---|---|---|---|
| Brewing method: | C; Single infusion mash, top fermented. | | |
| Mash liquor: | 9 litres | Alcohol content: | 3.3% |
| Mash temperature: | 63°C | Final gravity: | 1008 |
| Mash time: | 90 minutes | Bitterness: | 15 EBU |
| Boil time: | 90 minutes | Final volume: | 23 litres |

NOTES

All the colour in Everard's mild is added in the form of caramel. The black malt is added to compensate.

MALT EXTRACT VERSION – Partial mash required

Replace the pale malt with 2,200 grams of diastatic malt extract such as EDME DMS. Brew using Malt Extract Brewing – Method B.

# Highgate MILD

A beautifully-made, luscious dark mild from the Highgate brewery in Walsall, West Midlands, a subsidary of Bass. Chewy malt and light fruit with dry-nutty finish.

Classification:    English Cask-Conditioned Mild Ale

Original gravity:          1035.5

*In the mash tun*

| | | |
|---|---|---|
| Mild ale malt: | 2,800 g | (70%) |
| Crystal malt: | 400 g | (10%) |
| Black malt: | 80 g | (2%) |
| Torrefied barley: | 240 g | (6%) |

*In the copper*

| | | |
|---|---|---|
| Glucose syrup: | 470 g | (12%) |
| Goldings hops: | 55 g | (start of boil) |
| Goldings hops: | 10 g | (last 15 minutes) |

*Typical characteristics*

| | | | |
|---|---|---|---|
| Brewing method: | C; Single infusion mash, top fermented. | | |
| Mash liquor: | 9 litres | Alcohol content: | 3.6% |
| Mash temperature: | 63°C | Final gravity: | 1009 |
| Mash time: | 90 minutes | Bitterness: | 22 EBU |
| Boil time: | 90 minutes | Final volume: | 23 litres |

## NOTES

The Highgate brewery is unique, in that it only produces mild ale and the occasional Christmas Old Ale.

MALT EXTRACT VERSION – Partial mash required

Replace the pale malt with 2,000 grams of diastatic malt extract such as EDME DMS. Brew using Malt Extract Brewing – Method B.

# Higson's BEST MILD

Dark ruby beer from Whitbread's Exchange Brewery in Sheffield. Some nuttiness in the mouth, short finish.

Classification:   English Cask-Conditioned Mild Ale

Original gravity:          1032

*In the mash tun*

| | | |
|---|---|---|
| Mild ale malt: | 2,500 g | (70%) |
| Crystal malt: | 220 g | (6%) |
| Torrefied wheat: | 350 g | (10%) |
| Chocolate malt: | 140 g | (4%) |

*In the copper*

| | | |
|---|---|---|
| Invert cane sugar: | 350 g | (10%) |
| Fuggles hops: | 18 g | (start of boil) |
| Styrian Goldings: | 8 g | (start of boil) |
| Challenger hops: | 10 g | (start of boil) |
| British Columbian hops: | 6 g | (start of boil) |
| Fuggles hops: | 10 g | (last 15 minutes) |

*Typical characteristics*

Brewing method:      C, Single infusion mash, top fermented.

| | | | |
|---|---|---|---|
| Mash liquor: | 8 litres | Alcohol content: | 3.5% |
| Mash temperature: | 63°C | Final gravity: | 1006 |
| Mash time: | 90 minutes | Bitterness: | 22 EBU |
| Boil time: | 90 minutes | Final volume: | 23 litres |

NOTES

Whitbread add caramel for colour in this particular brew. They use a whirlpool, and therefore add their hops in pellet form.

# Holden's BLACK COUNTRY MILD

A splendid, tasty dark mild, full of malt and hop character, from Holden's brewery, Dudley, in the heart of the Black Country, a beer drinker's mecca. Inviting aroma of malt, with wholemeal biscuit notes. Chewy malt and roast in the mouth, dry hoppy finish.

Classification:   English Cask-Conditioned Mild Ale

Original gravity:          1037

*In the mash tun*

| | | |
|---|---|---|
| Mild ale malt: | 3,700 g | (90%) |
| Roast barley: | 210 g | (5%) |

*In the copper*

| | | |
|---|---|---|
| Invert cane sugar: | 210 g | (5%) |
| Fuggles hops: | 33 g | (start of boil) |
| Goldings hops: | 28 g | (start of boil) |
| Goldings hops: | 10 g | (last 15 minutes) |

*Typical characteristics*

| | | | |
|---|---|---|---|
| Brewing method: | C, Single infusion mash, top fermented. | | |
| Mash liquor: | 10 litres | Alcohol content: | 3.9% |
| Mash temperature: | 63°C | Final gravity: | 1008 |
| Mash time: | 90 minutes | Bitterness: | 24 EBU |
| Boil time: | 90 minutes | Final volume: | 23 litres |

MALT EXTRACT VERSION – No mashing required

Replace the mild ale malt with 2,700 grams of non-diastatic, dark-coloured, malt extract and brew using Malt Extract Brewing – Method A.

# Home Brewery MILD

A smooth, easy-drinking dark mild from the Home Brewery in Nottingham, a subsidiary of Scottish & Newcastle. Inviting aromas of black chocolate and light hop. Nutty, chewy malt with dry finish and roast, and chocolate hints.

Classification:    English Cask-Conditioned Mild Ale

Original gravity:        1036

*In the mash tun*

| | | |
|---|---|---|
| Pale malt: | 2,500 g | (62%) |
| Crystal malt: | 600 g | (15%) |
| Black malt: | 180 g | (5%) |
| Flaked maize: | 310 g | (8%) |

*In the copper*

| | | |
|---|---|---|
| Invert cane sugar: | 390 g | (10%) |
| Target hops: | 5 g | (start of boil) |
| Fuggles hops: | 22 g | (start of boil) |
| Northdown hops: | 9 g | (start of boil) |
| Styrian goldings: | 8 g | (start of boil) |
| Fuggles hops: | 10 g | (last 15 minutes) |

*Typical characteristics*

| | | | |
|---|---|---|---|
| Brewing method: | C; Single infusion mash, top fermented. | | |
| Mash liquor: | 9 litres | Alcohol content: | 3.8% |
| Mash temperature: | 63°C | Final gravity: | 1008 |
| Mash time: | 90 minutes | Bitterness: | 22 EBU |
| Boil time: | 90 minutes | Final volume: | 23 litres |

MALT EXTRACT VERSION – Partial mash required

Replace the pale malt with 1,850 grams of diastatic malt extract such as EDME DMS. Brew using Malt Extract Brewing – Method B.

# Hook Norton BEST MILD

A distinctive and tasty light mild from the Hook Norton brewery in Oxfordshire. Malt in the mouth with a good hop finish and some fruit notes.

Classification:    English Cask-Conditioned Mild Ale

Original gravity:          1032

*In the mash tun*

| | | |
|---|---|---|
| Pale malt: | 3,350 g | (93%) |
| Flaked maize: | 220 g | (6%) |
| Black malt: | 35 g | (1%) |

*In the copper*

| | | |
|---|---|---|
| Challenger hops: | 18 g | (start of boil) |
| Fuggles hops: | 15 g | (start of boil) |
| Golding hops: | 13 g | (start of boil) |
| Goldings hops: | 13 g | (last 15 minutes) |
| Irish moss: | 1 tsp | (last 15 minutes) |

*Typical characteristics*

| | | | |
|---|---|---|---|
| Brewing method: | C; Single infusion mash, top fermented. | | |
| Mash liquor: | 9 litres | Alcohol content: | 3.2% |
| Mash temperature: | 63°C | Final gravity: | 1008 |
| Mash time: | 90 minutes | Bitterness: | 22 EBU |
| Boil time: | 90 minutes | Final volume: | 23 litres |

NOTES

Hook Norton add caramel for colour. The black malt has been added to compensate for this.

MALT EXTRACT VERSION – Partial mash required

Replace the pale malt with 2,450 grams of diastatic malt extract such as EDME DMS. Brew using Malt Extract Brewing – Method B.

# McMullen's AK

A superb, tasty, well-attenuated ale from McMullen's Hertford brewery. Marketed now as a pale ale, though it originated as a light mild. Sweet malt, fruit, and delicate hop in mouth, good dry finish with orange peel and faint chocolate notes.

Classification:    English Cask-Conditioned Mild Ale

Original gravity:          1033

*In the mash tun*

| | | |
|---|---|---|
| Pale malt: | 2,800 g | (79%) |
| Flaked maize: | 210 g | (6%) |
| Chocolate malt: | 35 g | (1%) |

*In the copper*

| | | |
|---|---|---|
| Invert sugar: | 250 g | (7%) |
| Glucose syrup: | 250 g | (7%) |
| Whitbread Goldings hops: | 44 g | (start of boil) |
| Irish moss: | 1 tsp | (last 15 minutes) |

*Typical characteristics*

| | | | |
|---|---|---|---|
| Brewing method: | C; Single infusion mash, top fermented. | | |
| Mash liquor: | 8 litres | Alcohol content: | 3.6% |
| Mash temperature: | 63°C | Final gravity: | 1006 |
| Mash time: | 90 minutes | Bitterness: | 22 EBU |
| Boil time: | 90 minutes | Final volume: | 23 litres |

MALT EXTRACT VERSION – Partial mash required

Replace the pale malt with 2,050 grams of diastatic malt extract such as EDME DMS. Brew using Malt Extract Brewing – Method B.

# Sarah Hughes DARK RUBY MILD

Superb dark brown beer with a gravity that recalls milds of the nineteenth century. Brewed at the Beacon Hotel, Sedgley, West Midlands to a Victorian recipe. At OG 1058 it should dispel any myth that mild is supposed to be weak. Rich, mouth-filling malt and hops, intense dry finish with tannin and fruit.

Classification:    English Cask-Conditioned Mild Ale

Original gravity:          1058

*In the mash tun*

| | | |
|---|---|---|
| Pale malt: | 5,000 g | (75%) |
| Crystal malt: | 1,650 g | (25%) |

*In the copper*

| | | |
|---|---|---|
| Fuggles hops: | 41 g | (start of boil) |
| Goldings hops: | 35 g | (start of boil) |
| Goldings hops: | 20 g | (last 15 minutes) |

*Typical characteristics*

| | | | |
|---|---|---|---|
| Brewing method: | C; Single infusion mash, top fermented. | | |
| Mash liquor: | 16 litres | Alcohol content: | 5.9% |
| Mash temperature: | 68°C | Final gravity: | 1014 |
| Mash time: | 2 hours | Bitterness: | 30 EBU |
| Boil time: | 2 hours | Final volume: | 23 litres |

MALT EXTRACT VERSION – No mashing required

Replace the pale malt with 3,650 grams of non-diastatic, malt extract and brew using Malt Extract Brewing – Method A.

# Daniel Thwaites BEST MILD

Superb dark mild with great depth from Thwaites Blackburn brewery. Rich malt and light nut aromas.

Classification:   English Cask-Conditioned Mild Ale

Original gravity:        1034

*In the mash tun*

| | | |
|---|---|---|
| Pale malt: | 2,600 g | (70%) |
| Crystal malt: | 600 g | (15%) |
| Chocolate malt: | 150 g | (4%) |

*In the copper*

| | | |
|---|---|---|
| Maltose syrup: | 420 g | (11%) |
| Fuggles hops: | 31 g | (start of boil) |
| Goldings hops: | 26 g | (start of boil) |
| Goldings hops: | 15 g | (last 15 minutes) |

*Typical characteristics*

| | | | |
|---|---|---|---|
| Brewing method: | C; Single infusion mash, top fermented. | | |
| Mash liquor: | 8 litres | Alcohol content: | 3.4% |
| Mash temperature: | 63°C | Final gravity: | 1009 |
| Mash time: | 90 minutes | Bitterness: | 22 EBU |
| Boil time: | 90 minutes | Final volume: | 23 litres |

MALT EXTRACT VERSION – No mashing required

Replace the pale malt with 1,900 grams of non-diastatic, malt extract and brew using Malt Extract Brewing – Method A.

# 12 Pale Ale and Bitter Recipes

> *It is impossible to realise that Burton is a town with breweries in it; the inevitable impression is that Burton consists of a congeries of breweries, around which a town exists on sufferance.... As I approached the portals of Bass, I did not exactly pause owing to my tread being on an Empires dust, but I moved on with reverential interest, by reason that I was in the confines of the birthplace of a world's beer. The birthplace of a hero, the nursery in which my bosom friend had spent his childhood's happy hours.*
>
> *- A Visit to Burton, 1871, Bass Museum.*

In the early days of commercial brewing, malt was kilned on a perforated floor with a fire burning underneath. Traditionally this fire would be composed of hardwoods, hornbeam being the preferred wood, but oak, ash, beech or apple were sometimes used; indeed the oak chippings from cask-making were often used.

The fuels used created plenty of smoke, which percolated through the perforated floor and smoked the malt. Smoking was considered to be an essential part of malting and added to the flavour, in much the same way as meat and fish are smoked today; and of course whisky malts are still smoked. Smoking made the traditional brown malts, which made brown ales. Indeed, if you could buy brown malt today, you would expect it to be smoked; technically, a brown ale should be made from *smoked brown* malt, irrespective of the actual colour of the beer. At one time, almost all beers were brown beers.

Pale ale, however, is made from pale malt, which is unsmoked. Pale malt was originally kilned over charcoal which burned cleanly and did not smoke the malt. It could therefore produce a lighter coloured, cleaner tasting beer. However, charcoal was expensive and huge quantities were required to kiln modest amounts of malt. Pale ales were therefore very expensive and were drunk only by the wealthy. Coal could also be used to produce pale malt, but again it was much more expensive than wood. Coal was expensive to mine, heavy, it had to be transported long distances, and it attracted a coal tax. Before the advent of the canal network, coal was impractical for most breweries.

In the early 1800s, Mark Hodgson, a London brewer, learned that outward-bound freight charges to India were very low. The Anglo-Indian trade was mostly homeward-bound and, as the ships were often forced to travel to India empty, he reasoned that he could supply the Indian market at a reasonable price. He chose to brew pale ale for this venture, presumably because he felt that his customers would be the rather upper-crust hierarchy of the British army who could afford, and would appreciate, the more expensive pale ales.

The Burton brewers were not the sort to miss a trick. They had been exporting their brown ale to Russia for years and they wanted to cash in on the Indian market. They made several attempts to imitate Mark Hodgson's ale, but failed and gave up the idea. Things came to a head in 1822 when the Russians suddenly slapped a high import duty on English ale. The Burton brewers were then forced to find alternative markets or die; many of them died. However, the East India Shipping Company suggested to Samuel Allsopp, a Burton brewer, that he brew a pale ale for the Indian market. Allsopp had attempted to brew pale ale before and failed, but nevertheless he had another try.

It is not clear why the Burton brewers had such difficulty in producing pale ale; it had been around for more than one hundred years by 1822. Obidia Poundage, a London brewer, stated that about 1710: "for the Gentry residing in London was introduced the pale ales they were habituated to in the country". The fact that they were brewed for the gentry probably reflects the high cost of pale malt. However, the first pale ale to be produced in Burton-upon-Trent was brewed in 1822 by Job Goodhead, head brewer of Allsopp's brewery – in a teapot! Bass started brewing pale ale the following year, and the Indian market was opened to the two major Burton brewers. The ale was named East India Pale Ale because it was brewed under contract to the East India Shipping Company.

As mentioned earlier, pale malt required coal for the kilns. The most economical method of conveying coal in the days before the railways was by canal; in fact, the coal barons of the time built and owned most of them. Access to cheap coal and coke gave the brewers access to pale malt, therefore the first breweries to specialise in pale ale were those sited beside canals. Bass of Burton, Allsopp of Burton, Joules of Stone, and Flowers of Stratford were some of the most famous pale ale brewers, and all had access to the canal network. This not only gave them access to coal, but also provided them with the means of transporting their pale ale to their markets.

Eventually coal tax was reduced. The industrialisation of Britain required plentiful supplies of coal at a reasonable price, and the extraction of coal gas provided coke as one of its by-products. By kilning the malt over coke a much lighter and cleaner pale malt could be produced. All of this had the effect of lowering the cost of pale ale in comparison to the more conventional beers, and a home market for pale ale developed. Many breweries across the country began to brew pale ale for the home market, although the Burton brewers reigned supreme.

From about 1830 onwards English Pale Ale swept across the country and then across the world. Brewing became Britain's second largest industry, second only to cotton. By about 1850 the importation of British beer was putting a considerable strain on the balance of payments of most countries and trade barriers aimed at British beer began to spring up in the affected countries. Some countries were unable to do this openly either owing to trade agreements or to the fact that their economies were dependant upon Britain and they could not risk reprisals.

The French, in characteristic style, started a smear campaign against British beer, probably because it was seriously affecting the French wine industry. In 1852 a certain M. Payer, a French government chemist, publicly declared that the British brewers were using strychnine as a hop substitute. The French strychnine manufacturers backed up his claim by confirming that they did indeed export considerable quantities of strychnine to the brewers of Burton-upon-Trent. Other French scientists claimed that it was impossible to make beers of such soundness and clarity without the use of strychnine. This was all eventually disproved, but the row did considerable damage to the reputation of British beer, both at home and abroad.

The importation of British beer was, no doubt, a major economic problem to the French, and being just across the channel it was easily obtainable and safer to drink than the local water, and probably their wine. British beer was probably France's largest non-convertible import. It was imported, imbibed, and then presumably "gardez-voused" out of the window in the classic French manner.

Although many breweries across the country took to brewing pale ale, Bass grew to be the largest and most famous. James Herbert who referred to himself as a "Practical Brewer of Burton-upon-Trent", stated in 1871 that the Burton brewers achieve the soft agreeable flavour to their ales by never boiling their worts hard. They used higher quantities of hops and merely simmered them for an extended period of three hours or more. However, Bass were certainly not simmering their ales by 1887, they were boiling them vigorously, although they were still boiling them for three hours. A modern pale ale would be boiled vigorously for about 1½ to 2 hours.

# Adnams SOUTHWOLD BITTER

A distinctive, generously-hopped, aromatic beer from Adnams Sole Bay Brewery in Suffolk. Malt underlaid by good hop balance, long bitter-sweet finish with citric fruit and hop resin notes. It also happens to be Roger Protz's favourite tipple.

Classification:   English Cask-Conditioned Bitter

Original gravity:        1036

*In the mash tun*

| | | |
|---|---|---|
| Pale malt: | 3,400 g | (86%) |
| Chocolate malt: | 75 g | (2%) |

*In the copper*

| | | |
|---|---|---|
| Maltose syrup: | 470 g | (12%) |
| Challenger hops: | 32 g | (start of boil) |
| Fuggles hops: | 37 g | (start of boil) |
| Goldings hops: | 15 g | (last 15 minutes) |
| Irish moss: | 1 tsp | (last 15 minutes) |

*Typical characteristics*

| | | | |
|---|---|---|---|
| Brewing method: | C; Single infusion mash, top fermented. | | |
| Mash liquor: | 9 litres | Alcohol content: | 3.7% |
| Mash temperature: | 65°C | Final gravity: | 1009 |
| Mash time: | 90 minutes | Bitterness: | 35 EBU |
| Boil time: | 2 hours | Final volume: | 23 litres |

## NOTES

Adnams were not particularly forthcoming about their recipe. Indeed it is only in a publication intended for foreign eyes that they confess to using brewing sugars and caramel for colouring. The chocolate malt is added for colour adjustment to replace the caramel.

MALT EXTRACT VERSION – No mash required

Replace the pale malt with 2,500 grams of non-diastatic, medium coloured malt extract. Brew using Malt Extract Brewing – Method A.

# Archer's BEST BITTER

An uncompromisingly hoppy beer and a fine thirst quencher from Archer's Swindon brewery. A good companion for ripe cheese. Tart and tangy malt and hops in the mouth, dry quenching finish with some citric notes.

Classification:   English Cask-Conditioned Pale Ale

Original gravity:          1040

*In the mash tun*

| | | |
|---|---|---|
| Pale malt: | 4,300 g | (95%) |
| Crystal malt: | 230 g | (5%) |

*In the copper*

| | | |
|---|---|---|
| Progress hops: | 44 g | (start of boil) |
| Fuggles hops: | 40 g | (start of boil) |
| East Kent Goldings: | 13 g | (last 15 minutes) |
| Irish moss: | 1 tsp | (last 15 minutes) |

*Typical characteristics*

| | | | |
|---|---|---|---|
| Brewing method: | C; Single infusion mash, top fermented. | | |
| Mash liquor: | 11 litres | Alcohol content: | 4.0% |
| Mash temperature: | 66°C | Final gravity: | 1011 |
| Mash time: | 90 minutes | Bitterness: | 36 EBU |
| Boil time: | 2 hours | Final volume: | 23 litres |

NOTES
Archer's use pellets for the East Kent Golding late hops.

MALT EXTRACT VERSION – No mash required

Replace the pale malt with 3,150 grams of non-diastatic, light-coloured malt extract. Brew using Malt Extract Brewing – Method A.

# Archer's GOLDEN BITTER

A pale, strong ale with fine balance of malt, hops and fruit from Archer's Swindon brewery. Malty in the mouth with deep intense finish. Strong hop character and light fruit.

Classification:    English Cask-Conditioned Pale Ale.

Original gravity:        1046

*In the mash tun*

Pale malt:              5200 g    (100%)

*In the copper*

| | | |
|---|---|---|
| Progress hops: | 43 g | (start of boil) |
| Whitbread Golding hops: | 28 g | (start of boil) |
| East Kent Goldings: | 15 g | (last 15 minutes) |
| Irish moss: | 1 tsp | (last 15 minutes) |

*Typical characteristics*

| | | | |
|---|---|---|---|
| Brewing method: | C; Single infusion mash, top fermented. | | |
| Mash liquor: | 13 litres | Alcohol content: | 4.7% |
| Mash temperature: | 66°C | Final gravity: | 1011 |
| Mash time: | 90 minutes | Bitterness: | 36 EBU |
| Boil time: | 2 hours | Final volume: | 23 litres |

NOTES
Archer's use pellets for the East Kent Golding late hops.

# Arkells 3B

A superb and memorable amber beer from Arkell's Swindon brewery. Delicate, beautifully-balanced malt and hop with lingering dry finish and hint of nut.

Classification:          English Cask-Conditioned Pale Ale

Original gravity:        1040

*In the mash tun*

| | | |
|---|---|---|
| Pale malt: | 4,000 g | (88%) |
| Crystal malt: | 450 g | (10%) |

*In the copper*

| | | |
|---|---|---|
| Maltose syrup: | 90 g | (2%) |
| Progress hops: | 40 g | (start of boil) |
| Goldings hops: | 25 g | (start of boil) |
| Fuggles hops: | 15 g | (last 15 minutes) |
| Irish moss: | 1 tsp | (last 15 minutes) |

*Typical characteristics*

| | | | |
|---|---|---|---|
| Brewing method: | C; Single infusion mash, top fermented. | | |
| Mash liquor: | 11 litres | Alcohol content: | 4.1% |
| Mash temperature: | 66°C | Final gravity: | 1010 |
| Mash time: | 90 minutes | Bitterness: | 30 EBU |
| Boil time: | 2 hours | Final volume: | 23 litres |

MALT EXTRACT VERSION – No mash required

Replace the pale malt with 2,950 grams of non-diastatic, light-coloured malt extract. Brew using Malt Extract Brewing – Method A.

# Arkell's KINGSDOWN ALE

A high quality ale, with a gravity approaching the quaffing ales of yester-year, from Arkell's Kingsdown brewery. Rich aromas of hop and ripe fruit. Ripe malt and fruit in the mouth, deep bitter-sweet finish with fruit notes.

Classification:     English Cask-Conditioned Pale Ale

Original gravity:         1052

*In the mash tun*

| | | |
|---|---|---|
| Pale malt: | 5,000 g | (86%) |
| Crystal malt: | 700 g | (12%) |

*In the copper*

| | | |
|---|---|---|
| Maltose syrup: | 120 g | (2%) |
| Progress hops: | 50 g | (start of boil) |
| Goldings hops: | 31 g | (start of boil) |
| Fuggles hops: | 15 g | (last 15 minutes) |
| Irish moss: | 1 tsp | (last 15 minutes) |

*Typical characteristics*

| | | | |
|---|---|---|---|
| Brewing method: | C; Single infusion mash, top fermented. | | |
| Mash liquor: | 14 litres | Alcohol content: | 5.3% |
| Mash temperature: | 66°C | Final gravity: | 1012 |
| Mash time: | 90 minutes | Bitterness: | 35 EBU |
| Boil time: | 2 hours | Final volume: | 23 litres |

MALT EXTRACT VERSION – No mash required

Replace the pale malt with 3,650 grams of non-diastatic, light-coloured malt extract. Brew using Malt Extract Brewing – Method A.

# Banks & Taylor SHEFFORD BITTER

A refreshing, well-hopped and tasty session bitter from Banks & Taylor's Shefford brewery in Bedfordshire. Light, clean grain and hop in the mouth with quenching bitter finish.

Classification:   English Cask-Conditioned Pale Ale

Original gravity:          1038

*In the mash tun*

| | | |
|---|---|---|
| Pale malt: | 4,000 g | (95%) |
| Crystal malt: | 220 g | (5%) |

*In the copper*

| | | |
|---|---|---|
| Challenger hops: | 65 g | (start of boil) |
| Fuggles hops: | 10 g | (last 15 minutes) |
| Goldings hops: | 10 g | (last 15 minutes) |

*Typical characteristics*

| | | | |
|---|---|---|---|
| Brewing method: | C; Single infusion mash, top fermented. | | |
| Mash liquor: | 11 litres | Alcohol content: | 3.9% |
| Mash temperature: | 65°C | Final gravity: | 1009 |
| Mash time: | 90 minutes | Bitterness: | 40 EBU |
| Boil time: | 2 hours | Final volume: | 23 litres |

MALT EXTRACT VERSION – No mash required

Replace the pale malt with 2,950 grams of non-diastatic, light-coloured malt extract. Brew using Malt Extract Brewing – Method A.

# Banks & Taylor SHEFFORD PALE ALE

A beautifully crafted, rounded ale. A fine companion for strong-flavoured food. From Banks & Taylor's Shefford brewery. Full, rounded malt and hops in the mouth, deep dry finish with fruit balance.

Classification:     English Cask-Conditioned Pale Ale

Original gravity:            1041

*In the mash tun*

| | | |
|---|---|---|
| Pale malt: | 4,000 g | (87%) |
| Crystal malt: | 330 g | (7%) |
| Wheat malt: | 280 g | (6%) |

*In the copper*

| | | |
|---|---|---|
| Fuggles hops: | 50 g | (start of boil) |
| Goldings hops: | 42 g | (start of boil) |
| Goldings hops: | 10 g | (last 15 minutes) |
| Irish moss: | 1 tsp | (last 15 minutes) |

*Typical characteristics*

| | | | |
|---|---|---|---|
| Brewing method: | C; Single infusion mash, top fermented. | | |
| Mash liquor: | 11 litres | Alcohol content: | 4.2% |
| Mash temperature: | 65°C | Final gravity: | 1010 |
| Mash time: | 90 minutes | Bitterness: | 36 EBU |
| Boil time: | 2 hours | Final volume: | 23 litres |

MALT EXTRACT VERSION – Partial mash required

Replace the pale malt with 2,950 grams of diastatic malt extract such as EDME DMS. Brew using Malt Extract Brewing – Method B.

# Banks & Taylor SHEFFORD OLD STRONG

A powerful, fruity strong ale from Banks & Taylor's Shefford brewery. Rich, mouth-filling grain with good bitter balance, intense finish with sultana and raisin notes.

Classification:    English Cask-Conditioned Pale Ale

Original gravity:        1050

*In the mash tun*

| Pale malt: | 5,400 g | (95%) |
|---|---|---|
| Crystal malt: | 280 g | (5%) |

*In the copper*

| Fuggles hops: | 52 g | (start of boil) |
|---|---|---|
| Goldings hops: | 45 g | (start of boil) |
| Goldings hops: | 15 g | (last 15 minutes) |
| Irish moss: | 1 tsp | (last 15 minutes) |

*Typical characteristics*

| Brewing method: | C; Single infusion mash, top fermented. | | |
|---|---|---|---|
| Mash liquor: | 14 litres | Alcohol content: | 5.1% |
| Mash temperature: | 66°C | Final gravity: | 1012 |
| Mash time: | 90 minutes | Bitterness: | 38 EBU |
| Boil time: | 2 hours | Final volume: | 23 litres |

MALT EXTRACT VERSION – No mash required

Replace the pale malt with 3,950 grams of non-diastatic, light-coloured malt extract. Brew using Malt Extract Brewing – Method A.

# Bass DRAUGHT BASS

The most widely available beer in Britain, brewed by Bass of Burton-upon-Trent, probably the most famous brewery in the world. Multi-layered mouth-feel, pronounced maltiness offset by delicate hop, long polished finish with apple notes.

Classification:    English Cask-Conditioned Pale Ale

Original gravity:         1043

*In the mash tun*

| | | |
|---|---|---|
| Pale malt: | 4,600 g | (95%) |
| Crystal malt: | 250 g | (5%) |

*In the copper*

| | | |
|---|---|---|
| Challenger hops: | 34 g | (start of boil) |
| Northdown hops: | 22 g | (start of boil) |
| Northdown hops: | 12 g | (last 15 minutes) |
| Irish moss: | 1 tsp | (last 15 minutes) |

*Typical characteristics*

Brewing method:      C; Single infusion mash, top fermented.

| | | | |
|---|---|---|---|
| Mash liquor: | 10 litres | Alcohol content: | 4.4% |
| Mash temperature: | 65°C | Final gravity: | 1010 |
| Mash time: | 90 minutes | Bitterness: | 35 EBU |
| Boil time: | 2 hours | Final volume: | 23 litres |

NOTES

This recipe has been included for completeness sake, but is more or less a calculated guess. Bass have a whirlpool and would therefore use hop pellets. Northern Brewer could be substituted for the Northdown. The notes that I have been given state that Draught Bass is not dry-hopped. However, the Bass of old certainly was. You may like to try dry-hopping with a couple of cones of Northdown or Northern Brewer.

MALT EXTRACT VERSION – No mash required

Replace the pale malt with 3,400 grams of non-diastatic, light-coloured malt extract. Brew using Malt Extract Brewing – Method A.

# Bass WORTHINGTON WHITE SHIELD

The classic India Pale Ale, a superb beer to drink on its own or with meat, fish and cheese dishes. Originally brewed at Burton-upon-Trent, but currently brewed at Bass's Hope Brewery in Sheffield. Malt and spice in the mouth, deep nutty finish with strong hop character and light apple fruit notes.

Classification:    English Bottle-Conditioned Pale Ale

Original gravity:         1051

*In the mash tun*

| | | |
|---|---|---|
| Pale malt: | 4,700 g | (85%) |
| Crystal malt: | 280 g | (5%) |

*In the copper*

| | | |
|---|---|---|
| Invert cane sugar: | 550 g | (10%) |
| Challenger hops: | 40 g | (start of boil) |
| Northdown hops: | 25 g | (start of boil) |
| Northdown hops: | 15 g | (last 15 minutes) |
| Irish moss: | 1 tsp | (last 15 minutes) |

*Typical characteristics*

| | | | |
|---|---|---|---|
| Brewing method: | C; Single infusion mash, top fermented. | | |
| Mash liquor: | 14 litres | Alcohol content: | 5.6% |
| Mash temperature: | 66°C | Final gravity: | 1009 |
| Mash time: | 90 minutes | Bitterness: | 40 EBU |
| Boil time: | 2 hours | Final Volume: | 23 litres |

NOTES

This recipe is more or less a calculated guess. I have used invert sugar in this recipe in order to make their published ABV tally with the calculated ABV. Bass occasionally use black malt for colour. Mature in barrel for three weeks before bottling and then condition in bottle for a further six weeks. Priming sugars should not be necessary.

# Bateman's XXXB BITTER

Superb, complex, premium bitter from George Bateman of Wainfleet. Four times winner of its class in the Champion Beer of Britain competition. Sweet malt in the mouth balanced by strong hop notes, deep rounded finish with strong hop presence and rich fruit.

Classification:     English Cask-Conditioned Bitter

Original gravity:            1048

*In the mash tun*

| | | |
|---|---|---|
| Pale malt: | 3,600 g | (72%) |
| Crystal malt: | 380 g | (7.5%) |
| Wheat flour: | 130 g | (2.5%) |

*In the copper*

| | | |
|---|---|---|
| Invert cane sugar: | 900 g | (18%) |
| Challenger hops: | 34 g | (start of boil) |
| Goldings hops: | 33 g | (start of boil) |
| Goldings hops: | 15 g | (last 15 minutes) |

*Typical characteristics*

| | | | |
|---|---|---|---|
| Brewing method: | C; Single infusion mash, top fermented. | | |
| Mash liquor: | 11 litres | Alcohol content: | 5.6% |
| Mash temperature: | 66°C | Final gravity: | 1006 |
| Mash time: | 90 minutes | Bitterness: | 35 EBU |
| Boil time: | 2 hours | Final volume: | 23 litres |

# Batham BEST BITTER

A straw-coloured, delectable and refreshing ale by Batham's Delph Brewery. Fine, sharp hop prickle in the mouth, intense dry finish with hop bitterness and light fruit.

Classification:     English Cask-Conditioned Pale Ale

Original gravity:          1043.5

*In the mash tun*

Pale malt:                 4,900 g     (100%)

*In the copper*

| | | |
|---|---|---|
| Fuggles hops: | 33 g | (start of boil) |
| Northdown hops: | 28 g | (start of boil) |
| Fuggles hops: | 12 g | (last 15 minutes) |
| Goldings hops: | 2 g | (dry hops in cask) |

*Typical characteristics*

| | | | |
|---|---|---|---|
| Brewing method: | C; Single infusion mash, top fermented. | | |
| Mash liquor: | 12 litres | Alcohol content: | 4.5% |
| Mash temperature: | 65°C | Final gravity: | 1010 |
| Mash time: | 90 minutes | Bitterness: | 30 EBU |
| Boil time: | 2 hours | Final volume: | 23 litres |

NOTES

A typical Black Country, no-nonsense approach to brewing. Pale malt, hops and nothing else, not only quality, but simplicity itself.

# Belhaven 80/-

A memorable, rounded ale with a complex mix of fruit and hop, from the Belhaven Brewery, Dunbar, Scotland. Mouth-filling balance of malt and tart fruit with intense dry finish.

Classification:    Scottish Cask-Conditioned Ale

Original gravity:          1041.5

*In the mash tun*

| | | |
|---|---|---|
| Pale malt: | 3,900 g | (86%) |
| Crystal malt: | 115 g | (2.5%) |
| Black malt: | 65 g | (1.5%) |

*In the copper*

| | | |
|---|---|---|
| Maltose syrup: | 450 g | (10%) |
| B.C. Bramlings: | 23 g | (start of boil) |
| Fuggles hops: | 31 g | (start of boil) |
| Goldings hops: | 12 g | (last 15 minutes) |
| Irish moss: | 1 tsp | (last 15 minutes) |

*Typical characteristics*

| | | | |
|---|---|---|---|
| Brewing method: | C; Single infusion mash, top fermented. | | |
| Mash liquor: | 10 litres | Alcohol content: | 4.2% |
| Mash temperature: | 65°C | Final gravity: | 1010 |
| Mash time: | 90 minutes | Bitterness: | 28 EBU |
| Boil time: | 2 hours | Final volume: | 23 litres |

MALT EXTRACT VERSION – No mash required

Replace the pale malt with 2,850 grams of non-diastatic, light-coloured malt extract. Brew using Malt Extract Brewing – Method A.

# BIG LAMP BITTER

A superb, beautifully balanced, copper coloured ale with plenty of hop and fruit character. Brewed by the Big Lamp Brewery of Newcastle-upon-Tyne. Rounded balance of malt and hop with deep, dry finish and orange peel notes.

Classification:    English Cask-Conditioned Pale Ale

Original gravity:            1040

*In the mash tun*

| | | |
|---|---|---|
| Pale malt: | 2,900 g | (70%) |
| Crystal malt: | 420 g | (10%) |

*In the copper*

| | | |
|---|---|---|
| Invert cane sugar: | 840 g | (20%) |
| Styrian Golding hops: | 27 g | (start of boil) |
| Fuggles hops: | 42 g | (start of boil) |
| East Kent Goldings: | 15 g | (last 15 minutes) |
| Irish moss: | 1 tsp | (last 15 minutes) |

*Typical characteristics*

| | | | |
|---|---|---|---|
| Brewing method: | C; Single infusion mash, top fermented. | | |
| Mash liquor: | 9 litres | Alcohol content: | 4.7% |
| Mash temperature: | 65°C | Final gravity: | 1006 |
| Mash time: | 90 minutes | Bitterness: | 30 EBU |
| Boil time: | 2 hours | Final volume: | 23 litres |

MALT EXTRACT VERSION – No mash required

Replace the pale malt with 2,150 grams of non-diastatic, medium-coloured malt extract. Brew using Malt Extract Brewing – Method A.

# Boddington's BITTER

A remarkable, light, golden bitter, a fine quenching session beer from Boddington's Strangeways Brewery, Manchester. Flinty dryness in the mouth, long, hard finish with hop bitterness and tart fruit.

Classification:    English Cask-Conditioned Pale Ale.

Original gravity:        1035

*In the mash tun*

| | | |
|---|---|---|
| Pale malt: | 3,700 g | (96.5%) |
| Black malt: | 20 g | (0.5%) |

*In the copper*

| | | |
|---|---|---|
| Cane sugar: | 120 g | (3%) |
| Fuggles hops: | 29 g | (start of boil) |
| Goldings hops: | 21 g | (start of boil) |
| Whitbread Golding hops: | 13 g | (start of boil) |
| Northern Brewer hops: | 3 g | (last 15 minutes) |
| Bramling Cross hops: | 5 g | (last 15 minutes) |
| East Kent Goldings: | 10 g | (last 15 minutes) |
| Irish moss: | 1 tsp | (last 15 minutes) |

*Typical characteristics*

| | | | |
|---|---|---|---|
| Brewing method: | C; Single infusion mash, top fermented. | | |
| Mash liquor: | 9 litres | Alcohol content: | 3.6% |
| Mash temperature: | 65°C | Final gravity: | 1008 |
| Mash time: | 90 minutes | Bitterness: | 30 EBU |
| Boil time: | 2 hours | Final volume: | 23 litres |

MALT EXTRACT VERSION – No mash required

Replace the pale malt with 2,700 grams of non-diastatic, medium-coloured malt extract. Brew using Malt Extract Brewing – Method A.

# Borve Brewery BORVE ALE

A fine, reddish-brown Scotch ale with deep malt and hop character from the Borve Brewery, Aberdeenshire. Rich, rounded malt with long, bitter finish and hint of chocolate.

Classification:     Scottish Cask-Conditioned Ale

Original gravity:          1040

*In the mash tun*

| | | |
|---|---|---|
| Pale malt: | 4,400 g | (97%) |
| Crystal malt: | 65 g | (1.5%) |
| Chocolate malt: | 22 g | (0.5%) |
| Roast barley: | 45 g | (1%) |

*In the copper*

| | | |
|---|---|---|
| Goldings hops: | 70 g | (start of boil) |
| Goldings hops: | 20 g | (last 15 minutes) |
| Irish moss: | 1 tsp | (last 15 minutes) |

*Typical characteristics*

Brewing method:     C; Single infusion mash, top fermented.

| | | | |
|---|---|---|---|
| Mash liquor: | 11 litres | Alcohol content: | 4.1% |
| Mash temperature: | 65°C | Final gravity: | 1010 |
| Mash time: | 90 minutes | Bitterness: | 30 EBU |
| Boil time: | 2 hours | Final volume: | 23 litres |

MALT EXTRACT VERSION – Partial mash required

Replace the pale malt with 3,200 grams of diastatic malt extract such as EDME DMS. Brew using Malt Extract Brewing – Method B.

# Brakspear BITTER (PA)

A superb, beautifully crafted, satisfying and refreshing bitter from Brakspear's Henley brewery. Full flavoured malt and hop flower in mouth, delicate, dry finish with massive hop flower character.

Classification:   English Cask-Conditioned Pale Ale

Original gravity:        1035

*In the mash tun*

| Pale malt: | 3,300 g | (85%) |
|---|---|---|
| Crystal malt: | 310 g | (8%) |
| Black malt: | 40 g | (2%) |

*In the copper*

| Invert cane sugar: | 240 g | (10%) |
|---|---|---|
| Fuggles hops: | 68 g | (start of boil) |
| Goldings hops: | 31 g | (start of boil) |
| Goldings hops: | 15 g | (last 15 minutes) |
| Irish moss: | 1 tsp | (last 15 minutes) |

*Typical characteristics*

| Brewing method: | C; Single infusion mash, top fermented. | | |
|---|---|---|---|
| Mash liquor: | 9 litres | Alcohol content: | 3.7% |
| Mash temperature: | 65°C | Final gravity: | 1007 |
| Mash time: | 90 minutes | Bitterness: | 38 EBU |
| Boil time: | 2 hours | Final volume: | 23 litres |

MALT EXTRACT VERSION – No mash required

Replace the pale malt with 2,400 grams of non-diastatic, light coloured malt extract. Brew using Malt Extract Brewing – Method A.

# Bunce's BENCHMARK

A light, refreshing bitter with a tart, aromatic and light fruit nose. Good malt feel in the mouth, fresh cleansing finish. Brewed by Bunce's Brewery, Netheravon, Wilts.

Classification:   English Cask-Conditioned Pale Ale

Original gravity:            1035

*In the mash tun*

| | | |
|---|---|---|
| Pale malt: | 3,300 g | (84%) |
| Crystal malt: | 300 g | (7.5%) |
| Brewer's wheat flour: | 340 g | (8.5%) |

*In the copper*

| | | |
|---|---|---|
| Challenger hops: | 37 g | (start of boil) |
| Goldings hops: | 36 g | (start of boil) |
| Goldings hops: | 12 g | (last 15 minutes) |
| Irish moss: | 1 tsp | (last 15 minutes) |

*Typical characteristics*

Brewing method:      C; Single infusion mash, top fermented.

| | | | |
|---|---|---|---|
| Mash liquor: | 10 litres | Alcohol content: | 3.6% |
| Mash temperature: | 65°C | Final gravity: | 1008 |
| Mash time: | 90 minutes | Bitterness: | 38 EBU |
| Boil time: | 2 hours | Final volume: | 23 litres |

MALT EXTRACT VERSION – Partial mash required

Replace the pale malt with 2,400 grams of diastatic malt extract such as EDME DMS. Brew using Malt Extract Brewing – Method B.

# Burton Bridge BITTER

A succulent and complex golden beer from the Burton Bridge Brewery at Burton-upon-Trent. Rich fruit and grain mouth feel with a deep, dry finish full of sultana notes.

Classification:    English Cask-Conditioned Pale Ale

Original gravity:        1042

*In the mash tun*

| | | |
|---|---|---|
| Pale malt: | 4,500 g | (95%) |
| Crystal malt: | 240 g | (5%) |

*In the copper*

| | | |
|---|---|---|
| Target hops: | 27 g | (start of boil) |
| Fuggles hops: | 44 g | (start of boil) |
| Fuggles hops: | 15 g | (last 15 minutes) |
| Styrian Golding hops: | 5 g | (dry hopped in cask) |

*Typical characteristics*

| | | | |
|---|---|---|---|
| Brewing method: | C; Single infusion mash, top fermented. | | |
| Mash liquor: | 12 litres | Alcohol content: | 4.3% |
| Mash temperature: | 66°C | Final gravity: | 1010 |
| Mash time: | 90 minutes | Bitterness: | 40 EBU |
| Boil time: | 2 hours | Final volume: | 23 litres |

# Burtonwood BEST BITTER

A delectable bitter with a fine, aromatic bouquet of hop resin and nutty malt. Mellow malt in the mouth with fruit notes, long finish full of hop and light fruit character. Brewed by Forshaw's Burtonwood brewery in Warrington.

Classification:    English Cask-Conditioned Pale Ale

Original gravity:        1036

*In the mash tun*

| | | |
|---|---|---|
| Pale malt: | 2,450 g | (65%) |
| Crystal malt: | 230 g | (6%) |
| Torrefied wheat: | 380 g | (10%) |

*In the copper*

| | | |
|---|---|---|
| Invert cane sugar: | 720 g | (19%) |
| Challenger hops: | 29 g | (start of boil) |
| Progress hops: | 18 g | (start of boil) |
| Fuggles hops: | 25 g | (start of boil) |
| Whitbread Golding hops: | 12 g | (last 15 minutes) |
| Irish moss: | 1 tsp | (last 15 minutes) |

*Typical characteristics*

| | | | |
|---|---|---|---|
| Brewing method: | C; Single infusion mash, top fermented. | | |
| Mash liquor: | 8 litres | Alcohol content: | 4.2% |
| Mash temperature: | 65°C | Final gravity: | 1005 |
| Mash time: | 90 minutes | Bitterness: | 36 EBU |
| Boil time: | 2 hours | Final volume: | 23 litres |

MALT EXTRACT VERSION – Partial mash required

Replace the pale malt with 1,800 grams of diastatic malt extract such as EDME DMS. Brew using Malt Extract Brewing – Method B.

# Caledonian 80/-

A superbly balanced golden heavy, 80 shilling is from the Caledonian Brewery in Edinburgh. Full malt in the mouth, deep, dry hop finish with chocolate notes.

Classification:   English Cask-Conditioned Pale Ale

Original gravity:          1043

*In the mash tun*

| | | |
|---|---|---|
| Pale malt: | 3,200 g | (65%) |
| Crystal malt: | 750 g | (15%) |
| Amber malt: | 500 g | (10%) |
| Chocolate malt: | 250 g | (5%) |
| Wheat malt: | 250 g | (5%) |

*In the copper*

| | | |
|---|---|---|
| Fuggles hops: | 50 g | (start of boil) |
| Goldings hops: | 42 g | (start of boil) |
| Goldings hops: | 7 g | (last 15 minutes) |
| Irish moss: | 1 tsp | (last 15 minutes) |

*Typical characteristics*

| | | | |
|---|---|---|---|
| Brewing method: | C; Single infusion mash, top fermented. | | |
| Mash liquor: | 12 litres | Alcohol content: | 4.3% |
| Mash temperature: | 65°C | Final gravity: | 1011 |
| Mash time: | 90 minutes | Bitterness: | 36 EBU |
| Boil time: | 2 hours | Final volume: | 23 litres |

MALT EXTRACT VERSION – Partial mash required

Replace the pale malt and amber malt with a total of 2,700 grams of diastatic malt extract, such as EDME DMS. Brew using Malt Extract Brewing – Method B.

# Cameron's STRONGARM

A beautifully crafted and complex ale from Cameron's Hartlepool brewery. Round malt and fruit with long dry finish and vanilla hints.

Classification:    English Cask-Conditioned Bitter

Original gravity:        1040

*In the mash tun*

| | | |
|---|---|---|
| Pale malt: | 2,700 g | (62%) |
| Crystal malt: | 700 g | (16%) |
| Flaked maize: | 350 g | (8%) |

*In the copper*

| | | |
|---|---|---|
| Maltose syrup: | 600 g | (14%) |
| Fuggles hops: | 90 g | (start of boil) |
| Goldings hops: | 15 g | (last 15 minutes) |
| Irish moss: | 1 tsp | (last 15 minutes) |

*Typical characteristics*

| | | | |
|---|---|---|---|
| Brewing method: | C; Single infusion mash, top fermented. | | |
| Mash liquor: | 10 litres | Alcohol content: | 4.1% |
| Mash temperature: | 65°C | Final gravity: | 1010 |
| Mash time: | 90 minutes | Bitterness: | 32 EBU |
| Boil time: | 2 hours | Final volume: | 23 litres |

NOTES
Cameron's uses a whirlpool and would therefore use hop pellets.

MALT EXTRACT VERSION – Partial mash required

Replace the pale malt with a total of 2,000 grams of diastatic malt extract, such as EDME DMS. Brew using Malt Extract Brewing – Method B.

# Cameron's TRADITIONAL BITTER

A tangy quaffing beer from Cameron's Brewery in Hartlepool, Cleveland. Light balance of malt and hop with long, dry finish and fruit notes.

Classification:   English Bottle-Conditioned Pale Ale

Original gravity:          1036

*In the mash tun*

| | | |
|---|---|---|
| Pale malt: | 2,800 g | (72%) |
| Crystal malt: | 270 g | (7%) |
| Flaked maize: | 350 g | (9%) |

*In the copper*

| | | |
|---|---|---|
| Maltose syrup: | 470 g | (12%) |
| Fuggles hops: | 90 g | (start of boil) |
| Goldings hops: | 10 g | (last 15 minutes) |
| Irish moss: | 1 tsp | (last 15 minutes) |

*Typical characteristics*

| | | | |
|---|---|---|---|
| Brewing method: | C; Single infusion mash, top fermented. | | |
| Mash liquor: | 9 litres | Alcohol content: | 3.7% |
| Mash temperature: | 65°C | Final gravity: | 1009 |
| Mash time: | 90 minutes | Bitterness: | 32 EBU |
| Boil time: | 2 hours | Final volume: | 23 litres |

NOTES
Cameron's uses a whirlpool therefore their hops would be added in pellet form.

# Castle Eden CASTLE EDEN ALE

A refreshing, medium strength ale from Whitbread's Castle Eden brewery in Hartlepool. Rich malt and fruit with delicate dry hoppy finish. An excellent accompaniment to a ploughman's lunch.

Classification:     English Cask-Conditioned Pale Ale

Original gravity:          1040

*In the mash tun*

| | | |
|---|---|---|
| Pale malt: | 3,000 g | (70%) |
| Torrefied wheat: | 420 g | (10%) |
| Chocolate malt: | 40 g | (1%) |

*In the copper*

| | | |
|---|---|---|
| Invert sugar: | 380 g | (9%) |
| Glucose syrup: | 420 g | (10%) |
| Target hops: | 42 g | (start of boil) |
| Goldings hops: | 5 g | (dry hops in cask) |

*Typical characteristics*

| | | | |
|---|---|---|---|
| Brewing method: | C; Single infusion mash, top fermented. | | |
| Mash liquor: | 9 litres | Alcohol content: | 4.4% |
| Mash temperature: | 65°C | Final gravity: | 1008 |
| Mash time: | 90 minutes | Bitterness: | 38 EBU |
| Boil time: | 2 hours | Final volume: | 23 litres |

## NOTES

Whitbread add their hops in the form of 90% hop extract and 10% Target hop pellets. The hop pellets are used because some solid hop material needs to be present for good yeast performance. They also use a whirlpool for trub removal.

# Chester's BEST BITTER

A bitter that is light in colour and body, from Whitbread's Exchange brewery in Sheffield. Light balance of grain and hop with dry finish and vanilla notes.

Classification:     English Cask-Conditioned Bitter

Original gravity:          1033

*In the mash tun*

| | | |
|---|---|---|
| Pale malt: | 2,600 g | (72%) |
| Crystal malt: | 100 g | (3%) |
| Torrefied wheat: | 540 g | (15%) |

*In the copper*

| | | |
|---|---|---|
| Invert cane sugar: | 360 g | (10%) |
| Target hops: | 28 g | (start of boil) |
| Goldings hops: | 5 g | (last 15 minutes) |
| Irish moss: | 1 tsp | (last 15 minutes) |

*Typical characteristics*

| | | | |
|---|---|---|---|
| Brewing method: | C; Single infusion mash, top fermented. | | |
| Mash liquor: | 9 litres | Alcohol content: | 3.7% |
| Mash temperature: | 65°C | Final gravity: | 1006 |
| Mash time: | 90 minutes | Bitterness: | 25 EBU |
| Boil time: | 2 hours | Final volume: | 23 litres |

NOTES

All Whitbread Group beers use roughly the same grist and add their hops in the form of extracts. This beer is no exception; Whitbread use 85% hop extract and 20% Target hop pellets in the commercial version. The hop pellets are required because good yeast performance is not obtained if the hop content is supplied completely from extracts.

# Courage BEST BITTER

A ruby coloured, malt accented bitter from Courage's Bristol brewery. Malt and toffee notes in the mouth, dry finish with hop character.

Classification:   English Cask-Conditioned Pale Ale

Original gravity:         1039

*In the mash tun*

| | | |
|---|---|---|
| Pale malt: | 3,500 g | (82%) |
| Crystal malt: | 320 g | (7.5%) |
| Black malt: | 20 g | (0.5%) |

*In the copper*

| | | |
|---|---|---|
| Maltose syrup: | 430 g | (10%) |
| Target hops: | 24 g | (start of boil) |
| Styrian Golding hops: | 13 g | (start of boil) |
| Hallertau hops: | 5 g | (last 15 minutes) |
| Styrian Golding hops: | 5 g | (last 15 minutes) |
| Irish moss: | 1 tsp | (last 15 minutes) |
| Styrian Golding hops: | 5 g | (dry hopped in cask) |
| Hallertau hops: | 5 g | (dry hopped in cask) |

*Typical characteristics*

| | | | |
|---|---|---|---|
| Brewing method: | C; Single infusion mash, top fermented. | | |
| Mash liquor: | 10 litres | Alcohol content: | 4.0% |
| Mash temperature: | 66°C | Final gravity: | 1009 |
| Mash time: | 90 minutes | Bitterness: | 29 EBU |
| Boil time: | 2 hours | Final volume: | 23 litres |

NOTES
Courage have a very complex blend of hops in their beers – the above recipe is somewhat simplified. The information provided by Courage reads:
Blend of Halcyon and Pipkin pale malt, crystal malt, black malt for colour, brewing sugar. Blend of English Omega, Target, and Zenith; German Hallertau and Hersbrucker; and Yugoslav Styrian Goldings hop pellets; dry hopped with a blend of Hallertau and Styrians. 29 units of bitterness. So, there is plenty of room for experimentation by the bold. See also the notes overleaf accompanying Courage Director's Bitter.

# Courage DIRECTOR'S BITTER

A superb, full-drinking and intriguingly complex ale, excellent with traditional English dishes. Brewed at Courage's Bristol brewery. Rich and fruity in the mouth, intense bitter sweet finish.

Classification:    English Cask-Conditioned Pale Ale

Original gravity:          1046

*In the mash tun*

| | | |
|---|---|---|
| Pale malt: | 4,150 g | (82%) |
| Crystal malt: | 380 g | (7.5%) |
| Black malt: | 25 g | (0.5%) |

*In the copper*

| | | |
|---|---|---|
| Maltose syrup: | 500 g | (10%) |
| Target hops: | 28 g | (start of boil) |
| Styrian Golding hops: | 15 g | (start of boil) |
| Hallertau hops: | 6 g | (last 15 minutes) |
| Styrian Golding hops: | 6 g | (last 15 minutes) |
| Irish moss: | 1 tsp | (last 15 minutes) |
| Styrian Golding hops: | 5 g | (dry hopped in cask) |
| Hallertau hops: | 5 g | (dry hopped in cask) |

*Typical characteristics*

| | | | |
|---|---|---|---|
| Brewing method: | C; Single infusion mash, top fermented. | | |
| Mash liquor: | 11 litres | Alcohol content: | 4.7% |
| Mash temperature: | 66°C | Final gravity: | 1011 |
| Mash time: | 90 minutes | Bitterness: | 34 EBU |
| Boil time: | 2 hours | Final volume: | 23 litres |

NOTES

Courage Directors is parti-gyled with Courage Best Bitter, and therefore shares the same grist. In fact, the Bristol brewery practises high gravity brewing, whereby they brew only one high gravity beer (about OG 1053). This standard beer is then diluted at the casking stage with de-oxygenated and UV sterilised water. The only difference between the range beers is the amount of water and caramel added when they cask it. They also use a whirlpool and therefore use hop pellets. See Courage Best Bitter for the official recipe.

# Crouch Vale STRONG ANGLIAN ALE

A deceptively light bodied brew with sharp hop edge from the Crouch Vale Brewery near Chelmsford. Dry malt and hops in the mouth, intense dry finish.

Classification:   English Cask-Conditioned Pale Ale

Original gravity:         1048

*In the mash tun*

| | | |
|---|---|---|
| Pale malt: | 4,800 g | (88%) |
| Crystal malt: | 270 g | (5%) |
| Wheat malt: | 380 g | (7%) |

*In the copper*

| | | |
|---|---|---|
| Challenger hops: | 36 g | (start of boil) |
| Whitbread Goldings hops: | 29 g | (start of boil) |
| East Kent Goldings: | 15 g | (last 15 minutes) |
| Irish moss: | 1 tsp | (last 15 minutes) |

*Typical characteristics*

| | | | |
|---|---|---|---|
| Brewing method: | C; Single infusion mash, top fermented | | |
| Mash liquor: | 13 litres | Alcohol content: | 4.9% |
| Mash temperature: | 66°C | Final gravity: | 1012 |
| Mash time: | 90 minutes | Bitterness: | 37 EBU |
| Boil time: | 2 hours | Final volume: | 23 litres |

MALT EXTRACT VERSION – Partial mash required

Replace the pale malt with 3,500 grams of diastatic malt extract such as EDME DMS. Brew using Malt Extract Brewing – Method B.

# Donnington SBA

A succulent ale from the Donnington brewery, Stow-on-the-Wold. Rich, rounded balance of malt and hop, dry finish with hints of fruit. Good with ripe cheese.

Classification:   English Cask-Conditioned Pale Ale

Original gravity:          1044

*In the mash tun*

| | | |
|---|---|---|
| Pale malt: | 4,250 g | (89%) |
| Chocolate malt: | 45 g | (1%) |

*In the copper*

| | | |
|---|---|---|
| Invert cane sugar: | 475 g | (10%) |
| Fuggles hops: | 100 g | (start of boil) |
| Fuggles hops: | 20 g | (last 15 minutes) |
| Irish moss: | 1 tsp | (last 15 minutes) |

*Typical characteristics*

| | | | |
|---|---|---|---|
| Brewing method: | C; Single infusion mash, top fermented. | | |
| Mash liquor: | 10 litres | Alcohol content: | 4.9% |
| Mash temperature: | 66°C | Final gravity: | 1008 |
| Mash time: | 90 minutes | Bitterness: | 32 EBU |
| Boil time: | 2 hours | Final volume: | 23 litres |

MALT EXTRACT VERSION – No mash required

Replace the pale malt with 3,100 grams of non-diastatic, medium-coloured malt extract. Brew using Malt Extract Brewing – Method A.

# Eldridge Pope THOMAS HARDY'S COUNTRY BITTER

A well-balanced, lightly fruity beer from the Eldridge Pope brewery in Thomas Hardy's Dorchester. Full flavours of malt and hops, long finish with good hop character and a mellow fruitiness.

Classification:   English Cask-Conditioned Pale Ale

Original gravity:   1041

*In the mash tun*

| | | |
|---|---|---|
| Pale malt: | 3,600 g | (80%) |
| Crystal malt: | 450 g | (10%) |

*In the copper*

| | | |
|---|---|---|
| Maltose syrup: | 450 g | (10%) |
| Fuggles hops: | 38 g | (start of boil) |
| Goldings hops: | 32 g | (start of boil) |
| Goldings hops: | 10 g | (last 15 minutes) |
| Irish moss: | 1 tsp | (last 15 minutes) |

*Typical characteristics*

| | | | |
|---|---|---|---|
| Brewing method: | C; Single infusion mash, top fermented. | | |
| Mash liquor: | 10 litres | Alcohol content: | 4.2% |
| Mash temperature: | 65°C | Final gravity: | 1010 |
| Mash time: | 90 minutes | Bitterness: | 27 EBU |
| Boil time: | 2 hours | Final volume: | 23 litres |

## NOTES

*Too much liquor is bad, and leads to that horned man in the smoky house; but after all, many people haven't the gift of enjoying a wet, and since we be highly favoured with a power that way, we should make the most o't.*
*– Thomas Hardy.*

# Eldridge Pope ROYAL OAK

A deep amber ale of great complexity and character from the Eldridge Pope Brewery in Dorchester. Mouth-filling malt and fruit with delicate, dry, bitter-sweet finish with pronounced "pear drops" flavour.

Classification:    English Cask-Conditioned Pale Ale

Original gravity:        1048

*In the mash tun*

| | | |
|---|---|---|
| Pale malt: | 4,200 g | (80%) |
| Crystal malt: | 530 g | (10%) |

*In the copper*

| | | |
|---|---|---|
| Maltose syrup: | 530 g | (10%) |
| Fuggles hops: | 42 g | (start of boil) |
| Goldings hops: | 35 g | (start of boil) |
| Goldings hops: | 10 g | (last 15 minutes) |
| Irish moss: | 1 tsp | (last 15 minutes) |

*Typical characteristics*

| | | | |
|---|---|---|---|
| Brewing method: | C; Single infusion mash, top fermented. | | |
| Mash liquor: | 12 litres | Alcohol content: | 4.9% |
| Mash temperature: | 65°C | Final gravity: | 1011 |
| Mash time: | 90 minutes | Bitterness: | 30 EBU |
| Boil time: | 2 hours | Final volume: | 23 litres |

MALT EXTRACT VERSION – No mash required

Replace the pale malt with 3,100 grams of non-diastatic, medium-coloured malt extract. Brew using Malt Extract Brewing – Method A.

# Everard's BEACON BITTER

An amber ale, light and quaffable, from Everard's Leicester brewery.
Chewy malt character in mouth; light, dry finish.

Classification:   English Cask-Conditioned Pale Ale

Original gravity:          1036

*In the mash tun*

| | | |
|---|---|---|
| Pale malt: | 3,200 g | (80%) |
| Crystal malt: | 450 g | (11%) |
| Torrefied wheat: | 200 g | ( 5%) |

*In the copper*

| | | |
|---|---|---|
| Invert cane sugar: | 160 g | (4%) |
| Challenger hops: | 30 g | (start of boil) |
| Fuggles hops: | 17 g | (start of boil) |
| Goldings hops: | 12 g | (last 15 minutes) |
| Irish moss: | 1 tsp | (last 15 minutes) |

*Typical characteristics*

| | | | |
|---|---|---|---|
| Brewing method: | C; Single infusion mash, top fermented. | | |
| Mash liquor: | 10 litres | Alcohol content: | 3.8% |
| Mash temperature: | 65°C | Final gravity: | 1008 |
| Mash time: | 90 minutes | Bitterness: | 25 EBU |
| Boil time: | 2 hours | Final volume: | 23 litres |

MALT EXTRACT VERSION – Partial mash required

Replace the pale malt with 2,350 grams of diastatic malt extract such as
EDME DMS. Brew using Malt Extract Brewing – Method B.

# Everard's OLD ORIGINAL

An amber ale, light and quaffable, from Everard's Leicester brewery. Chewy malt character in mouth, light dry finish.

Classification:   English Cask-Conditioned Pale Ale

Original gravity:        1050

*In the mash tun*

| | | |
|---|---|---|
| Pale malt: | 4,500 g | (80%) |
| Crystal malt: | 840 g | (15%) |

*In the copper*

| | | |
|---|---|---|
| Invert cane sugar: | 140 g | (2.5%) |
| Maltose syrup: | 140 g | (2.5%) |
| Challenger hops: | 34 g | (start of boil) |
| Fuggles hops: | 20 g | (start of boil) |
| Goldings hops: | 15 g | (last 15 minutes) |
| Irish moss: | 1 tsp | (last 15 minutes) |
| Goldings hops: | 15 g | (dry hopped in cask) |

*Typical characteristics*

| | | | |
|---|---|---|---|
| Brewing method: | C; Single infusion mash, top fermented | | |
| Mash liquor: | 13 litres | Alcohol content: | 5.2% |
| Mash temperature: | 65°C | Final gravity: | 1011 |
| Mash time: | 90 minutes | Bitterness: | 28 EBU |
| Boil time: | 2 hours | Final volume: | 23 litres |

MALT EXTRACT VERSION – No mash required

Replace the pale malt with 3,300 grams of non-diastatic, medium-coloured malt extract. Brew using Malt Extract Brewing – Method A.

# Exe Valley BITTER

A pale amber beer from the Exe Valley Brewery near Exeter, with pleasing attraction of roast barley. Rich mouth feel of malt and roast barley; long, bitter finish with good nut character.

Classification:   English Cask-Conditioned Pale Ale

Original gravity:        1041.5

*In the mash tun*

| | | |
|---|---|---|
| Pale malt: | 4,450 g | (95%) |
| Roasted barley: | 230 g | (5%) |

*In the copper*

| | | |
|---|---|---|
| Fuggles hops: | 100 g | (start of boil) |
| Fuggles hops: | 15 g | (last 15 minutes) |

*Typical characteristics*

| | | | |
|---|---|---|---|
| Brewing method: | C; Single infusion mash, top fermented | | |
| Mash liquor: | 11 litres | Alcohol content: | 4.2% |
| Mash temperature: | 65°C | Final gravity: | 1010 |
| Mash time: | 90 minutes | Bitterness: | 35 EBU |
| Boil time: | 2 hours | Final volume: | 23 litres |

NOTES
Exe Valley Brewery's "Dolby's Bitter" is a similar beer but dry hopped. Try dry hopping with 5 grams of Fuggles.

Presumably Dolby's Bitter is a "low-noise" beer.

MALT EXTRACT VERSION – No mash required

Replace the pale malt with 3,250 grams of non-diastatic, medium-coloured malt extract. Brew using Malt Extract Brewing – Method A.

# Exmoor EXMOOR GOLD

A superb and quenching golden ale. Almost a hybrid, with a lager bouquet and palate, and with the finish of a strong ale. Dry, quenching balance of malt and hops, long finish with bitter-sweet notes and light fruit hints.

Classification: English Cask-Conditioned Pale Ale

Original gravity: 1045

*In the mash tun*

Pale malt: 5,000 g (100%)

*In the copper*

| | | |
|---|---|---|
| Fuggles hops: | 34 g | (start of boil) |
| Challenger hops: | 28 g | (start of boil) |
| Goldings hops: | 20 g | (start of boil) |
| Goldings hops: | 20 g | (last 15 minutes) |
| Irish moss: | 1 tsp | (last 15 minutes) |

*Typical characteristics*

| | | | |
|---|---|---|---|
| Brewing method: | C; Single infusion mash, top fermented | | |
| Mash liquor: | 12 litres | Alcohol content: | 4.6% |
| Mash temperature: | 66°C | Final gravity: | 1011 |
| Mash time: | 90 minutes | Bitterness: | 32 EBU |
| Boil time: | 2 hours | Final volume: | 23 litres |

# Federation SPECIAL ALE

A sweetish, malty brew with a chewy malt character and a delicate hop finish. Brewed by the Federation Brewery in Tyne and Wear. (I wonder if the Klingons have their own brewery as well!)

Classification:   English Cask-Conditioned Pale Ale

Original gravity:        1041

*In the mash tun*
Pale malt:              3,300 g    (75%)
Flaked maize:             440 g    (10%)

*In the copper*

Maltose syrup:            650 g    (15%)
Target hops:               20 g    (start of boil)
Challenger hops:           28 g    (start of boil)
Bramling Cross hops:       10 g    (last 15 minutes)
Irish moss:               1 tsp    (last 15 minutes)

*Typical characteristics*

Brewing method:       C; Single infusion mash, top fermented
Mash liquor:          10 litres         Alcohol content:   4.2%
Mash temperature:     65°C              Final gravity:     1010
Mash time:            90 minutes        Bitterness:        25 EBU
Boil time:            2 hours           Final volume:      23 litres

# Felinfoel DOUBLE DRAGON

A beautifully crafted, golden bitter from the Felinfoel Brewery in Dyfed, South Wales. Full malt and vinous fruit in mouth; deep, complex finish with hops, fruit and faint toffee notes.

Classification:   Welsh Cask-Conditioned Pale Ale

Original gravity:          1048

*In the mash tun*

| | | |
|---|---|---|
| Pale malt: | 4,150 g | (79%) |
| Crystal malt: | 160 g | (3%) |
| Torrefied wheat: | 530 g | (10%) |

*In the copper*

| | | |
|---|---|---|
| Invert cane sugar: | 425 g | (8%) |
| Challenger hops: | 20 g | (start of boil) |
| Bramling Cross hops: | 12 g | (start of boil) |
| Whitbread Golding hops: | 12 g | (start of boil) |
| Whitbread Golding: | 10 g | (last 15 minutes) |
| Irish moss: | 1 tsp | (last 15 minutes) |

*Typical characteristics*

| | | | |
|---|---|---|---|
| Brewing method: | C; Single infusion mash, top fermented | | |
| Mash liquor: | 12 litres | Alcohol content: | 5.3% |
| Mash temperature: | 66°C | Final gravity: | 1009 |
| Mash time: | 90 minutes | Bitterness: | 25 EBU |
| Boil time: | 2 hours | Final volume: | 23 litres |

NOTES
Felinfoel appear to have recently increased the gravity of this beer from 1040 to 1048.

MALT EXTRACT VERSION – Partial mash required

Replace the pale malt with 3,000 grams of diastatic malt extract such as EDME DMS. Brew using Malt Extract Brewing – Method B.

# Flowers ORIGINAL BITTER

A strong, fruity bitter with some acidity, from Whitbread's Cheltenham brewery. Fat malt in the mouth with hop edge, dry finish with some hop character with raisin and sultana notes.

Classification:   English Cask-Conditioned Pale Ale

Original gravity:           1044

*In the mash tun*

| | | |
|---|---|---|
| Pale malt: | 3,150 g | (65%) |
| Crystal malt: | 360 g | (7.5%) |
| Torrefied wheat: | 725 g | (15%) |

*In the copper*

| | | |
|---|---|---|
| Maltose syrup: | 600 g | (12.5%) |
| Target hops: | 31 g | (start of boil) |
| Styrian Goldings: | 3 g | (start of boil) |
| Styrian Goldings: | 10 g | (last 15 minutes) |
| Irish moss: | 1 tsp | (last 15 minutes) |
| Target hops: | 5 g | (dry hopped in cask) |

*Typical characteristics*

| | | | |
|---|---|---|---|
| Brewing method: | C; Single infusion mash, top fermented | | |
| Mash liquor: | 11 litres | Alcohol content: | 4.5% |
| Mash temperature: | 65°C | Final gravity: | 1010 |
| Mash time: | 90 minutes | Bitterness: | 30 EBU |
| Boil time: | 2 hours | Final volume: | 23 litres |

MALT EXTRACT VERSION – Partial mash required

Replace the pale malt with 2,300 grams of diastatic malt extract such as EDME DMS. Brew using Malt Extract Brewing – Method B.

# Fullers LONDON PRIDE

An astonishingly complex beer for its gravity, fine for drinking on its own or with well flavoured food. A multi layered delight of malt and hops and a deep, intense finish with hop and ripening fruit notes.

Classification:   English Cask-Conditioned Bitter

Original gravity:          1040

*In the mash tun*

| | | |
|---|---|---|
| Pale malt: | 2,750 g | (65%) |
| Crystal malt: | 430 g | (10%) |
| Flaked maize: | 430 g | (10%) |

*In the copper*

| | | |
|---|---|---|
| Invert cane sugar: | 640 g | (15%) |
| Target hops: | 20 g | (start of boil) |
| Challenger hops: | 20 g | (start of boil) |
| Northdown hops: | 9 g | (last 15 minutes) |
| Irish moss: | 1 tsp | (last 15 minutes) |

*Typical characteristics*

| | | | |
|---|---|---|---|
| Brewing method: | C; Single infusion mash, top fermented | | |
| Mash liquor: | 10 litres | Alcohol content: | 4.6% |
| Mash temperature: | 65°C | Final gravity: | 1006 |
| Mash time: | 90 minutes | Bitterness: | 30 EBU |
| Boil time: | 2 hours | Final volume: | 23 litres |

MALT EXTRACT VERSION – Partial mash required

Replace the pale malt with 2,000 grams of diastatic malt extract such as EDME DMS. Brew using Malt Extract Brewing – Method B.

# Gales HORNDEAN SPECIAL BITTER

A complex, slightly sour strong ale, from the Gales Horndean brewery near Portsmouth. Full malt with hop edge in the mouth, intense finish with citric and faint chocolate malts.

Classification:   English Cask-Conditioned Pale Ale

Original gravity:          1050

*In the mash tun*

| | | |
|---|---|---|
| Pale malt: | 4,000 g | (78.5%) |
| Torrefied wheat: | 260 g | (5%) |
| Black malt: | 75 g | (1.5%) |

*In the copper*

| | | |
|---|---|---|
| White sugar: | 770 g | (15%) |
| Challenger hops: | 20 g | (start of boil) |
| Goldings hops: | 22 g | (start of boil) |
| Fuggles hops: | 26 g | (start of boil) |
| Goldings hops: | 10 g | (last 15 minutes) |
| Irish moss: | 1 tsp | (last 15 minutes) |

*Typical characteristics*

| | | | |
|---|---|---|---|
| Brewing method: | C; Single infusion mash, top fermented | | |
| Mash liquor: | 11 litres | Alcohol content: | 5.8% |
| Mash temperature: | 65°C | Final gravity: | 1007 |
| Mash time: | 90 minutes | Bitterness: | 32 EBU |
| Boil time: | 2 hours | Final volume: | 23 litres |

MALT EXTRACT VERSION – Partial mash required

Replace the pale malt with 2,900 grams of diastatic malt extract such as EDME DMS. Brew using Malt Extract Brewing – Method B.

# Glenny Brewery WYCHWOOD BEST

A rounded, light copper ale from the Glenny brewery at Whitney in Oxfordshire. Full malt in the mouth with hop balance and rich fuity finish.

Classification:   English Cask-Conditioned Ale

Original gravity:         1044

*In the mash tun*

| | | |
|---|---|---|
| Pale malt: | 4,750 g | (96%) |
| Crystal malt: | 180 g | (3.75%) |
| Chocolate malt: | 12 g | (0.25%) |

*In the copper*

| | | |
|---|---|---|
| Progress hops: | 60 g | (start of boil) |
| Styrian Golding hops: | 12 g | (dry hopped in cask) |
| Irish moss: | 1 tsp | (last 15 minutes) |

*Typical characteristics*

| | | | |
|---|---|---|---|
| Brewing method: | C; Single infusion mash, top fermented | | |
| Mash liquor: | 12 litres | Alcohol content: | 4.5% |
| Mash temperature: | 65°C | Final gravity: | 1011 |
| Mash time: | 90 minutes | Bitterness: | 30 EBU |
| Boil time: | 2 hours | Final volume: | 23 litres |

MALT EXTRACT VERSION – No mash required

Replace the pale malt with 3,500 grams of non-diastatic, medium coloured malt extract. Brew using Malt Extract Brewing – Method A.

# Harviestoun Brewery ORIGINAL 80/-

A golden coloured quenching beer with a great hop character for a Scottish brew. Fruity in the mouth with good hop balance and long, dry finish.

Classification:   Scottish Cask-Conditioned Pale Ale

Original gravity:         1041

*In the mash tun*

| | | |
|---|---|---|
| Pale malt: | 3,600 g | (82%) |
| Crystal malt: | 350 g | (8%) |

*In the copper*

| | | |
|---|---|---|
| Soft brown sugar: | 440 g | (10%) |
| Fuggles hops: | 55 g | (start of boil) |
| Goldings hops: | 15 g | (last 15 minutes) |
| Irish moss: | 1 tsp | (last 15 minutes) |
| Styrian Goldings: | 10 g | (dry hopped in cask) |

*Typical characteristics*

| | | | |
|---|---|---|---|
| Brewing method: | C; Single infusion mash, top fermented | | |
| Mash liquor: | 10 litres | Alcohol content: | 4.6% |
| Mash temperature: | 65°C | Final gravity: | 1007 |
| Mash time: | 90 minutes | Bitterness: | 20 EBU |
| Boil time: | 2 hours | Final volume: | 23 litres |

MALT EXTRACT VERSION – No mash required

Replace the pale malt with 2,650 grams of non-diastatic, medium-coloured malt extract. Brew using Malt Extract Brewing – Method A.

# Home Brewery HOME BITTER

A copper coloured brew with good drinkability and quenching light fruitiness from the Home Brewery, Nottingham. Pleasing balance of malt and hop bitterness in mouth with dry finish and light fruit notes.

Classification:   English Cask-Conditioned Pale Ale.

Original gravity:        1038

*In the mash tun*

| | | |
|---|---|---|
| Pale malt: | 2,800 g | (70%) |
| Chocolate malt: | 80 g | (2%) |
| Flaked maize: | 640 g | (16%) |

*In the copper*

| | | |
|---|---|---|
| Maltose syrup: | 200g | (5%) |
| Cane sugar: | 280 g | (7%) |
| Fuggles hops: | 36 g | (start of boil) |
| Styrian Golding hops: | 15 g | (start of boil) |
| Irish moss: | 1 tsp | (last 15 minutes) |

*Typical characteristics*

| | | | |
|---|---|---|---|
| Brewing method: | C; Single infusion mash, top fermented | | |
| Mash liquor: | 9 litres | Alcohol content: | 4.0% |
| Mash temperature: | 65°C | Final gravity: | 1008 |
| Mash time: | 90 minutes | Bitterness: | 22 EBU |
| Boil time: | 2 hours | Final volume: | 23 litres |

MALT EXTRACT VERSION – Partial mash required

Replace the pale malt with 2,050 grams of diastatic malt extract such as EDME DMS. Brew using Malt Extract Brewing – Method B.

# Hook Norton BEST BITTER

A distinctive pale bitter with some fruity complexity from the Hook Norton brewery in Oxfordshire. Light, dry balance of grain and hop with delicate finish and some citric fruit notes.

Classification:   English Cask-Conditioned Pale Ale

Original gravity:         1036

*In the mash tun*

| | | |
|---|---|---|
| Pale malt: | 3,750 g | (92.5%) |
| Flaked maize: | 240 g | (6%) |
| Chocolate malt: | 60 g | (1.5%) |

*In the copper*

| | | |
|---|---|---|
| Fuggles hops: | 33 g | (start of boil) |
| Challenger hops: | 30 g | (start of boil) |
| Goldings hops: | 10 g | (last 15 minutes) |
| Irish moss: | 1 tsp | (last 15 minutes) |

*Typical characteristics*

| | | | |
|---|---|---|---|
| Brewing method: | C: Single infusion mash, top fermented | | |
| Mash liquor: | 10 litres | Alcohol content: | 3.7% |
| Mash temperature: | 65°C | Final gravity: | 1009 |
| Mash time: | 90 minutes | Bitterness: | 30 EBU |
| Boil time: | 2 hours | Final volume: | 23 litres |

MALT EXTRACT VERSION – Partial mash required

Replace the pale malt with 2,750 grams of diastatic malt extract such as EDME DMS. Brew using Malt Extract Brewing – Method B.

# Ind Coope BURTON ALE

A magnificent ale, full of character, from Ind Coope's Burton brewery. Great mouth filling balance of malt and hop with superb, memorably intense finish full of hops and fruit notes.

Classification:    English Cask-Conditioned Pale Ale

Original gravity:              1047.5

*In the mash tun*

| | | |
|---|---|---|
| Pale malt: | 4,500 g | (87.5%) |
| Chocolate malt: | 75 g | (1.5%) |

*In the copper*

| | | |
|---|---|---|
| Maltose syrup: | 570 g | (11%) |
| Target hops: | 40 g | (start of boil) |
| Styrian Golding hops: | 10 g | (last 15 minutes) |
| Irish moss: | 1 tsp | (last 15 minutes) |
| Styrian Goldings hops: | 10 g | (dry hopped in class) |

*Typical characteristics*

| | | | |
|---|---|---|---|
| Brewing method: | C: Single infusion mash, top fermented | | |
| Mash liquor: | 12 litres | Alcohol content: | 4.8% |
| Mash temperature: | 65°C | Final gravity: | 1012 |
| Mash time: | 90 minutes | Bitterness: | 35 EBU |
| Boil time: | 2 hours | Final volume | 23 litres |

NOTES

In the past, a Burton Ale referred to the brown ales that were made in Burton prior to 1822 and not pale ale. Brown ales were made from smoked brown malt.

MALT EXTRACT VERSION – Partial mash required

Replace the pale malt with 3,300 grams of diastatic malt extract such as EDME DMS. Brew using Malt Extract Brewing – Method B.

# Malton DOUBLE CHANCE BITTER

A pale coloured ale with a breathtaking bitter character from the Malton Brewery, in Malton, West Yorks. Superb balance of malt and light fruit with intense dry finish.

Classification:   English Cask-Conditioned Pale Ale

Original gravity:        1038

*In the mash tun*

| | | |
|---|---|---|
| Pale malt: | 4,000 g | (95%) |
| Crystal malt: | 215 g | (5%) |

*In the copper*

| | | |
|---|---|---|
| Goldings hops: | 64 g | (start of boil) |
| Goldings hops: | 15 g | (last 15 minutes) |
| Irish moss: | 1 tsp | (last 15 minutes) |

*Typical characteristics*

| | | | |
|---|---|---|---|
| Brewing method: | C: Single infusion mash, top fermented | | |
| Mash liquor: | 11 litres | Alcohol content: | 3.9% |
| Mash temperature: | 65°C | Final gravity: | 1009 |
| Mash time: | 90 minutes | Bitterness: | 27 EBU |
| Boil time: | 2 hours | Final volume: | 23 litres |

MALT EXTRACT VERSION – No mash required

Replace the pale malt with 2,950 grams of non-diastatic, medium coloured malt extract. Brew using Malt Extract Brewing – Method A.

115

# Marston BURTON BEST BITTER

A beautifully crafted, subtly deceptive Burton beer from Marston's Burton brewery. Superb balance of malt and hops with a long and delicate hop finish.

Classification:   English Cask-Conditioned Pale Ale

Original gravity:          1036

*In the mash tun*

| | | |
|---|---|---|
| Pale malt: | 3,100 g | (81%) |
| Chocolate malt: | 75 g | (2%) |

*In the copper*

| | | |
|---|---|---|
| Maltose syrup: | 650 g | (17%) |
| Fuggles hops: | 26 g | (start of boil) |
| Goldings hops: | 22 g | (start of boil) |
| Whitbread Goldings hops: | 19 g | (start of boil) |
| Goldings hops: | 10 g | (last 15 minutes) |
| Irish moss: | 1 tsp | (last 15 minutes) |

*Typical characteristics*

| | | | |
|---|---|---|---|
| Brewing method: | C: Single infusion mash, top fermented | | |
| Mash liquor: | 9 litres | Alcohol content: | 3.7% |
| Mash temperature: | 65°C | Final gravity: | 1009 |
| Mash time: | 90 minutes | Bitterness: | 28 EBU |
| Boil time: | 2 hours | Final volume: | 23 litres |

# Marston PEDIGREE BITTER

A lightly luscious beer from Marston's Burton brewery. The only beer still brewed using the famous "Burton Union" method, although sadly only for yeast propagation purposes. Stunning, multi layered and delicious light assault of malt and hops, with long, delicate finish full of delightful hop and apple notes with slight saltiness.

Classification:   English Cask-Conditioned Pale Ale

Original gravity:          1043

*In the mash tun*

| | | |
|---|---|---|
| Pale malt: | 3,700 g | (81%) |
| Chocolate malt: | 90 g | (2%) |

*In the copper*

| | | |
|---|---|---|
| Maltose syrup: | 800 g | (17%) |
| Fuggles hops: | 30 g | (start of boil) |
| Goldings hops: | 26 g | (start of boil) |
| Whitbread Goldings hops: | 23 g | (start of boil) |
| Goldings hops: | 10 g | (last 15 minutes) |
| Irish moss: | 1 tsp | (last 15 minutes) |

*Typical characteristics*

| | | | |
|---|---|---|---|
| Brewing method: | C: Single infusion mash, top fermented | | |
| Mash liquor: | 10 litres | Alcohol content: | 4.4% |
| Mash temperature: | 65°C | Final gravity: | 1010 |
| Mash time: | 90 minutes | Bitterness: | 30 EBU |
| Boil time: | 2 hours | Final volume: | 23 litres |

MALT EXTRACT VERSION – Partial mash required

Replace the pale malt with 2,700 grams of diastatic malt extract such as EDME DMS. Brew using Malt Extract Brewing – Method B.

# McMullen's COUNTRY BEST BITTER

A bitter from McMullen's Hertford brewery with a brilliant balance of malt and hop character. Full, mouth filling malt, deep, dry finish with pronounced fruit and vanilla notes.

Classification:   English Cask-Conditioned Pale Ale

Original gravity:          1041

*In the mash tun*

| | | |
|---|---|---|
| Pale malt: | 3,350 g | (76%) |
| Crystal malt: | 180 g | (4%) |
| Flaked maize: | 260 g | (6%) |

*In the copper*

| | | |
|---|---|---|
| Maltose syrup: | 620 g | (14%) |
| Whitbread Goldings hops: | 60 g | (start of boil) |
| Irish moss: | 1 tsp | (last 15 minutes) |
| Whitbread Goldings hops: | 10 g | (dry hopped in cask) |

*Typical characteristics*

| | | | |
|---|---|---|---|
| Brewing method: | C: Single infusion mash, top fermented | | |
| Mash liquor: | 14 litres | Alcohol content: | 4.2% |
| Mash temperature: | 65°C | Final gravity: | 1010 |
| Mash time: | 90 minutes | Bitterness: | 30 EBU |
| Boil time: | 2 hours | Final volume: | 23 litres |

# Moorhouse's PENDLE WITCHES BREW

A deceptively pale strong bitter, dangerously potable. From Moorhouse's brewery in Burnley. Sweet grain in the mouth, deep, dry finish with good hop character and vanilla notes.

Classification:   English Cask-Conditioned Pale Ale

Original gravity:          1050

*In the mash tun*

| | | |
|---|---|---|
| Pale malt: | 5,200 g | (92%) |
| Crystal malt: | 225 g | (4%) |
| Flaked maize: | 225 g | (4%) |

*In the copper*

| | | |
|---|---|---|
| Fuggles hops: | 97 g | (start of boil) |
| Fuggles hops: | 20 g | (last 15 minutes) |
| Irish moss: | 1 tsp | (last 15 minutes) |

*Typical characteristics*

| | | | |
|---|---|---|---|
| Brewing method: | C; Single infusion mash, top fermented | | |
| Mash liquor: | 14 litres | Alcohol content: | 5.1% |
| Mash temperature: | 66°C | Final gravity: | 1012 |
| Mash time: | 90 minutes | Bitterness: | 35 EBU |
| Boil time: | 2 hours | Final volume: | 23 litres |

MALT EXTRACT VERSION – Partial mash required

Replace the pale malt with 3,800 grams of diastatic malt extract such as EDME DMS. Brew using Malt Extract Brewing – Method B.

# Morrells VARSITY BITTER

A rich and satisfying ale, good for drinking on its own or through a meal. Full-tasting malt and hop in the mouth, deep, bitter sweet finish with hints of vanilla.

Classification:    English Cask-Conditioned Bitter
Original gravity:            1041

*In the mash tun*
Pale malt:                3,750 g    (80%)
Crystal malt:               470 g    (10%)
Torrefied wheat:            470 g    (10%)

*In the copper*

Challenger hops:             50 g    (start of boil)
Goldings hops:               15 g    (last 15 minutes)
Irish moss:                 1 tsp    (last 15 minutes)
Goldings hops:                5 g    (dry hops in cask)

*Typical characteristics*

Brewing method:        C; Single infusion mash, top fermented

| Mash liquor: | 11 litres | Alcohol content: | 4.2% |
|---|---|---|---|
| Mash temperature: | 65°C | Final gravity: | 1010 |
| Mash time: | 90 minutes | Bitterness: | 31 EBU |
| Boil time: | 2 hours | Final volume | 23 litres |

# Nethergate BITTER

A succulent, coppery ale from the Nethergate brewery in Sudbury whose full palate suggests a greater gravity. Rich and rounded balance of malt and hops, deep finish with fruit hints. Excellent with fish or cheese.

Classification:   English Cask-Conditioned Pale Ale

Original gravity:          1039

*In the mash tun*

| | | |
|---|---|---|
| Pale malt: | 3,900 g | (88.5%) |
| Crystal malt: | 220 g | (5%) |
| Black malt: | 65 g | (1.5%) |
| Wheat flour: | 220 g | (5%) |

*In the copper*

| | | |
|---|---|---|
| Whitbread Golding hops: | 70 g | (start of boil) |
| Fuggles hops: | 15 g | (last 15 minutes) |
| Irish moss: | 1 tsp | (last 15 minutes) |
| Fuggles hops: | 5 g | (dry hopped in cask) |

*Typical characteristics*

| | | | |
|---|---|---|---|
| Brewing method: | C; Single infusion mash, top fermented | | |
| Mash liquor: | 11 litres | Alcohol Content: | 3.9% |
| Mash temperature: | 65°C | Final gravity: | 1010 |
| Mash time: | 90 minutes | Bitterness: | 36 EBU |
| Boil time: | 2 hours | Final volume: | 23 litres |

MALT EXTRACT VERSION – Partial mash required

Replace the pale malt with 2,850 grams of diastatic malt extract such as EDME DMS. Brew using Malt Extract Brewing – Method B.

# Reepham RAPIER PALE ALE

A ripe, rounded, good-drinking, pale golden bitter from the Reepham brewery in Norfolk. Full, rich grain in the mouth, deep dry finish.

Classification:   English Cask-Conditioned Pale Ale

Original gravity:        1044

*In the mash tun*

| | | |
|---|---|---|
| Pale malt: | 4,300 g | (87%) |
| Crystal malt: | 395 g | (8%) |
| Wheat flour: | 50 g | (1%) |

*In the copper*

| | | |
|---|---|---|
| Barley syrup: | 200 g | (4%) |
| Golding hops: | 33 g | (start of boil) |
| Fuggles hops: | 38 g | (start of boil) |
| Fuggles hops: | 15 g | (last 15 minutes) |
| Irish moss: | 1 tsp | (last 15 minutes) |
| Fuggles hops: | 5 g | (dry hopped in cask) |

*Typical characteristics*

| | | | |
|---|---|---|---|
| Brewing method: | C; Single infusion mash, top fermented | | |
| Mash liquor: | 12 litre | Alcohol content: | 4.5% |
| Mash temperature: | 65°C | Final gravity: | 1011 |
| Mash time: | 90 minutes | Bitterness: | 28 EBU |
| Boil time: | 2 hours | Final volume: | 23 litres |

# Ringwood OLD THUMPER

A warm, rounded, yet surprisingly delicate pale strong beer from Ringwood Brewery in Hampshire. Voted Champion Beer of Britain in 1988. Luscious balance of grain and hop in the mouth, bitter-sweet finish with pronounced hop aftertaste.

Classification:   English Cask-Conditioned Pale Ale

Original gravity:          1058

*In the mash tun*

| | | |
|---|---|---|
| Pale malt: | 5,800 g | (90%) |
| Crystal malt: | 250 g | (4%) |
| Flaked wheat: | 125 g | (2%) |

*In the copper*

| | | |
|---|---|---|
| Maltose syrup: | 260 g | (4%) |
| Challenger hops: | 34 g | (start of boil) |
| Progress hops: | 42 g | (start of boil) |
| East Kent Goldings: | 18 g | (last 15 minutes) |
| Irish moss: | 1 tsp | (last 15 minutes) |

*Typical characteristics*

| | | | |
|---|---|---|---|
| Brewing method: | C; Single infusion mash, top fermented | | |
| Mash liquor: | 15 litres | Alcohol content: | 5.9% |
| Mash temperature: | 66°C | Final gravity: | 1014 |
| Mash time: | 90 minutes | Bitterness: | 42 EBU |
| Boil time: | 2 hours | Final volume: | 23 litres |

NOTE

You can convert this recipe into Ringwood Fortyniner (OG 1048) by dividing all of the ingredients by 1.2, including the hops. For quality control purposes, you can taste the real thing in The Inn on the Furlong, in Ringwood.

# Ruddles COUNTY

A rich and tasty ale from Ruddles Oakham brewery. Mouth filling and complex balance of grain, fruit and hop with deep, rounded, dry fruit finish. A fine companion for a tangy ploughman's lunch.

Classification:   English Cask-Conditioned Pale Ale

Original gravity:         1050

*In the mash tun*

| | | |
|---|---|---|
| Pale malt: | 4,650 g | (85%) |
| Crystal malt: | 220 g | (4%) |

*In the copper*

| | | |
|---|---|---|
| Maltose syrup: | 600 g | (11%) |
| Challenger hops: | 31 g | (start of boil) |
| Northdown hops: | 30 g | (start of boil) |
| Goldings hops: | 20 g | (last 15 minutes) |
| Irish moss: | 1 tsp | (last 15 minutes) |

*Typical characteristics*

| | | | |
|---|---|---|---|
| Brewing method: | C; Single infusion mash, top fermented | | |
| Mash liquor: | 12 litres | Alcohol content: | 5.1% |
| Mash temperature: | 66°C | Final gravity: | 1012 |
| Mash time: | 90 minutes | Bitterness: | 38 EBU |
| Boil time: | 2 hours | Final volume: | 23 litres |

MALT EXTRACT VERSION – No mash required

Replace the pale malt with 3,400 grams of non-diastatic, medium coloured malt extract. Brew using Malt Extract Brewing – Method A.

# Samuel Smith's OLD BREWERY BITTER

A full flavoured and woody bitter from Sam Smith's Tadcaster brewery. Full malt and fruit on tongue, light dry, finish with vanilla notes.

Classification:   English Cask-Conditioned Pale Ale

Original gravity:        1037

*In the mash tun*

| | | |
|---|---|---|
| Pale malt: | 3,800 g | (91%) |
| Crystal malt: | 380 g | (9%) |

*In the copper*

| | | |
|---|---|---|
| Fuggles hops: | 75 g | (start of boil) |
| Goldings hops: | 15 g | (last 15 minutes) |
| Irish moss: | 1 tsp | (last 15 minutes) |

*Typical characteristics*

Brewing method:        C; Single infusion mash, top fermented

| | | | |
|---|---|---|---|
| Mash liquor: | 10 litres | Alcohol content: | 3.8% |
| Mash temperature: | 65°C | Final gravity: | 1009 |
| Mash time: | 90 minutes | Bitterness: | 27 EBU |
| Boil time: | 2 hours | Final volume: | 23 litres |

MALT EXTRACT VERSION – No mash required

Replace the pale malt with 2,700 grams of non-diastatic, medium-coloured malt extract.  Brew using Malt Extract Brewing – Method A.

# Shepherd Neame MASTERBREW BEST BITTER

A big, bold beer full of delectable hop character, from Shepherd Neame's Faversham brewery. Good balance of malt and fruit in the mouth, intense, dry finish with citric fruit notes.

Classification:   English Cask-Conditioned Pale Ale

Original gravity:          1036

*In the mash tun*

| | | |
|---|---|---|
| Pale malt: | 2,800 g | (70%) |
| Amber malt: | 200 g | (5%) |
| Crystal malt: | 280 g | (7%) |
| Wheat malt: | 160 g | (4%) |
| Torrefied wheat: | 240 g | (6%) |

*In the copper*

| | | |
|---|---|---|
| Maltose syrup: | 320 g | (8%) |
| Target hops: | 25 g | (start of boil) |
| Goldings hops: | 13 g | (start of boil) |
| Goldings hops: | 12 g | (last 15 minutes) |
| Irish moss: | 1 tsp | (last 15 minutes) |
| Goldings hops: | 5 g | (dry hopped in cask) |

*Typical characteristics*

| | | | |
|---|---|---|---|
| Brewing method: | C; Single infusion mash, top fermented | | |
| Mash liquor: | 10 litres | Alcohol content: | 3.7% |
| Mash temperature: | 65°C | Final gravity: | 1009 |
| Mash time: | 90 minutes | Bitterness: | 28 EBU |
| Boil time: | 2 hours | Final volume: | 23 litres |

NOTES

Shepherd Neame use Golding hop oil to achieve hoppy aroma.

# Smiles BREWERY BITTER

A golden quaffing bitter from Smiles Bristol brewery. Ripe malt in the mouth, long finish with hops, fruit and nuts.

Classification:   English Cask-Conditioned Pale Ale

Original gravity:         1037

*In the mash tun*

| | | |
|---|---|---|
| Pale malt: | 3,800 g | (90%) |
| Amber malt: | 420 g | (10%) |

*In the copper*

| | | |
|---|---|---|
| Goldings hops: | 66 g | (start of boil) |
| Goldings hops: | 12 g | (last 15 minutes) |
| Irish moss: | 1 tsp | (last 15 minutes) |

*Typical characteristics*

| | | | |
|---|---|---|---|
| Brewing method: | C; Single infusion mash, top fermented | | |
| Mash liquor: | 10 litres | Alcohol content: | 3.8% |
| Mash temperature: | 65°C | Final gravity: | 1009 |
| Mash time: | 90 minutes | Bitterness: | 28 EBU |
| Boil time: | 2 hours | Final volume: | 23 litres |

# Stones BEST BITTER

A delectable, straw coloured bitter from the old Stones brewery in Sheffield, part of Bass. Delicate straw on tongue with mellow, bitter finish.

Classification:   English Cask-Conditioned Pale Ale

Original gravity:          1038

*In the mash tun*

| | | |
|---|---|---|
| Pale malt: | 3,150 g | (79%) |
| Crystal malt: | 40 g | (1%) |

*In the copper*

| | | |
|---|---|---|
| Maltose syrup: | 800 g | (20%) |
| Challenger hops: | 27 g | (start of boil) |
| Northdown hops: | 25 g | (start of boil) |
| Goldings hops: | 10 g | (start of boil) |
| Goldings hops: | 15 g | (last 15 minutes) |
| Irish moss: | 1 tsp | (last 15 minutes) |
| Goldings hops: | 4 g | (dry hopped in cask) |

*Typical characteristics*

| | | | |
|---|---|---|---|
| Brewing method: | C; Single infusion mash, top fermented | | |
| Mash liquor: | 9 litres | Alcohol content: | 3.9% |
| Mash temperature: | 65°C | Final gravity: | 1009 |
| Mash time: | 90 minutes | Bitterness: | 28 EBU |
| Boil time: | 2 hours | Final volume: | 23 litres |

MALT EXTRACT VERSION – No mash required

Replace the pale malt with 2,300 grams of non-diastatic, medium coloured malt extract. Brew using Malt Extract Brewing – Method A.

# Tetley BITTER

A superb tangy bitter. Smooth mouth filling balance of malt and hops with deep dry finish and lingering fruit notes.

Classification:   English Cask-Conditioned Pale Ale

Original gravity:          1035.5

*In the mash tun*

| | | |
|---|---|---|
| Pale malt: | 2,900 g | (74.5%) |
| Torrefied barley: | 390 g | (10%) |
| Chocolate malt: | 20 g | (0.5%) |

*In the copper*

| | | |
|---|---|---|
| Maltose syrup: | 580 g | (15%) |
| Target hops: | 28 g | (start of boil) |
| Northdown hops: | 15 g | (last 15 minutes) |
| Northdown hops: | 5 g | (dry hops in cask) |
| Irish moss: | 1 tsp | (last 15 minutes) |

*Typical characteristics*

| | | | |
|---|---|---|---|
| Brewing method: | C; Single infusion mash, top fermented | | |
| Mash liquor: | 11 litres | Alcohol content: | 3.6% |
| Mash temperature: | 65°C | Final gravity: | 1009 |
| Mash time: | 90 minutes | Bitterness: | 25 EBU |
| Boil time: | 2 hours | Final volume: | 23 litres |

## NOTES

Tetley actually use micronised barley; the torrefied barley is used here as a substitute. Micronised cereals are very finely ground; almost to a flour. Micronised barley is unlikely to be found in our home brewing shops, and as Tetley is the only brewer in this book that uses the stuff, it would be unfair to expect home brew shops to stock it; hence the substitution. The chocolate malt is added for colouring. Tetley add caramel for colour.

# Theakston's BEST BITTER

Pale bitter with distinctive hop flower character; quenching and lightly fruity. Delicate bitter sweet balance in the mouth, light dry finish with good hop character.

Classification:   English Cask-Conditioned Pale Ale

Original gravity:        1038

*In the mash tun*

| | | |
|---|---|---|
| Pale malt: | 2,900 g | (74%) |
| Crystal malt: | 200 g | (5%) |
| Flaked maize: | 320 g | (8%) |

*In the copper*

| | | |
|---|---|---|
| Cane sugar: | 510 g | (13%) |
| Target hops: | 13 g | (start of boil) |
| Fuggles hops: | 33 g | (start of boil) |
| Goldings hops: | 15 g | (last 15 minutes) |
| Irish moss: | 1 tsp | (last 15 minutes) |

*Typical characteristics*

| | | | |
|---|---|---|---|
| Brewing method: | C; Single infusion mash, top fermented | | |
| Mash liquor: | 10 litres | Alcohol content: | 4.4% |
| Mash temperature: | 65°C | Final gravity: | 1006 |
| Mash time: | 90 minutes | Bitterness: | 24 EBU |
| Boil time: | 2 hours | Final volume: | 23 litres |

MALT EXTRACT VERSION – Partial mash required

Replace the pale malt with 2,100 grams of diastatic malt extract such as EDME DMS. Brew using Malt Extract Brewing – Method B.

# Timothy Taylor BEST BITTER

A golden bitter of exceptional quality and drinkability. Full and complex grain and fruit with deep dry nutty finish.

Classification:  English Cask-Conditioned Pale Ale
Original gravity:        1037

*In the mash tun*

| | | |
|---|---|---|
| Pale malt: | 3,600 g | (85%) |
| Crystal malt: | 630 g | (15%) |

*In the copper*

| | | |
|---|---|---|
| Goldings hops: | 28 g | (start of boil) |
| Fuggles hops: | 30 g | (start of boil) |
| Styrian Goldings: | 16 g | (start of boil) |
| Goldings hops: | 15 g | (last 15 minutes) |
| Irish moss: | 1 tsp | (last 15 minutes) |

*Typical characteristics*

| | | | |
|---|---|---|---|
| Brewing method: | C; Single infusion mash, top fermented | | |
| Mash liquor: | 10 litres | Alcohol content: | 3.8% |
| Mash temperature: | 66°C | Final gravity: | 1009 |
| Mash time: | 90 minutes | Bitterness: | 30 EBU |
| Boil time: | 2 hours | Final volume: | 23 litres |

MALT EXTRACT VERSION – No mash required

Replace the pale malt with 2,600 grams of non-diastatic, medium coloured malt extract. Brew using Malt Extract Brewing – Method A.

# Timothy Taylor LANDLORD

A superb beer of enormous character and complexity, from the Knowle Spring Brewery in Keighley. Stunning, mouth filling, multi layered interweaving of malt and hop with intense hop and fruit finish.

Classification:   English Cask-Conditioned Pale Ale

Original gravity:          1042

*In the mash tun*

Pale malt:                 4,700 g     (100%)

*In the copper*

| | | |
|---|---|---|
| Goldings hops: | 28 g | (start of boil) |
| Fuggles hops: | 50 g | (start of boil) |
| Goldings hops: | 15 g | (last 15 minutes) |
| Irish moss: | 1 tsp | (last 15 minutes) |

*Typical characteristics*

| | | | |
|---|---|---|---|
| Brewing method: | C; Single infusion mash, top fermented | | |
| Mash liquor: | 11 litres | Alcohol content: | 4.3% |
| Mash temperature: | 66°C | Final gravity: | 1010 |
| Mash time: | 90 minutes | Bitterness: | 30 EBU |
| Boil time: | 2 hours | Final volume: | 23 litres |

# Titanic LIFEBOAT ALE

A dark and tasty, full bodied brew from the Titanic brewery, Stoke-on-Trent. Sweet malt in the mouth, dry, malty finish with some fruit notes.

Classification:   English Cask-Conditioned Pale Ale

Original gravity:          1040

*In the mash tun*

| | | |
|---|---|---|
| Pale malt: | 3,900 g | (85%) |
| Crystal malt: | 640 g | (14%) |
| Black malt: | 45 g | (1%) |

*In the copper*

| | | |
|---|---|---|
| Goldings hops: | 13 g | (start of boil) |
| Fuggles hops: | 62 g | (start of boil) |
| Goldings hops: | 15 g | (last 15 minutes) |
| Irish moss: | 1 tsp | (last 15 minutes) |

*Typical characteristics*

| | | | |
|---|---|---|---|
| Brewing method: | C; Single infusion mash, top fermented | | |
| Mash liquor: | 11 litres | Alcohol content: | 4.1% |
| Mash temperature: | 65°C | Final gravity: | 1010 |
| Mash time: | 90 minutes | Bitterness: | 28 EBU |
| Boil time: | 2 hours | Final volume: | 23 litres |

MALT EXTRACT VERSION – No mash required

Replace the pale malt with 2,850 grams of non-diastatic, medium- coloured malt extract. Brew using Malt Extract Brewing – Method A.

# Tolly Cobbold BITTER

A tasty, tangy bitter of distinction from Tolly's Ipswich brewery. Complex balance of malt in mouth and intense, dry finish.

Classification:   English Cask-Conditioned Pale Ale

Original gravity:       1035

*In the mash tun*

| | | |
|---|---|---|
| Pale malt: | 3,000 g | (75%) |
| Amber malt: | 400 g | (10%) |
| Crystal malt: | 600 g | (15%) |

*In the copper*

| | | |
|---|---|---|
| Goldings hops: | 62 g | (start of boil) |
| Goldings hops: | 12 g | (last 15 minutes) |
| Irish moss: | 1 tsp | (last 15 minutes) |

*Typical characteristics*

| | | | |
|---|---|---|---|
| Brewing method: | C; Single infusion mash, top fermented | | |
| Mash liquor: | 10 litres | Alcohol content: | 3.6% |
| Mash temperature: | 65°C | Final gravity: | 1009 |
| Mash time: | 90 minutes | Bitterness: | 26 EBU |
| Boil time: | 2 hours | Final volume: | 23 litres |

# Wadworth's 6X

A copper coloured, rounded ale of enormous depth and quality from Wadworth's Devizes brewery. Complex, bitter sweet palate, long, dry finish with vanilla notes.

Classification:   English Cask-Conditioned Pale Ale

Original gravity:        1040

*In the mash tun*

| | | |
|---|---|---|
| Pale malt: | 3,900 g | (89%) |
| Crystal malt: | 130 g | (3%) |

*In the copper*

| | | |
|---|---|---|
| Invert cane sugar: | 350 g | (8%) |
| Fuggles hops: | 61 g | (start of boil) |
| Irish moss: | 1 tsp | (last 15 minutes) |
| Goldings hops: | 4 g | (dry hops in cask) |

*Typical characteristics*

| | | | |
|---|---|---|---|
| Brewing method: | C; Single infusion mash, top fermented | | |
| Mash liquor: | 10 litres | Alcohol content: | 4.4% |
| Mash temperature: | 65°C | Final gravity: | 1008 |
| Mash time: | 90 minutes | Bitterness: | 22 EBU |
| Boil time: | 2 hours | Final volume: | 23 litres |

MALT EXTRACT VERSION – No mash required

Replace the pale malt with 2,850 grams of non-diastatic, medium coloured malt extract. Brew using Malt Extract Brewing – Method A.

# Wiltshire STONEHENGE BEST BITTER

A pale, full-flavoured bitter that suggests a stronger gravity. Brewed at the Stonehenge Brewery, Tisbury. Ripe malt and fruit in the mouth, deep finish with hop and fruit character.

Classification:   English Cask-Conditioned Pale Ale

Original gravity:        1040

*In the mash tun*

| | | |
|---|---|---|
| Pale malt: | 4,100 g | (90%) |
| Crystal malt: | 225 g | (5%) |
| Amber malt: | 25 g | (5%) |

*In the copper*

| | | |
|---|---|---|
| Fuggles hops: | 33 g | (start of boil) |
| Goldings hops: | 38 g | (start of boil) |
| Goldings hops: | 15 g | (last 15 minutes) |
| Irish moss: | 1 tsp | (last 15 minutes) |

*Typical characteristics*

| | | | |
|---|---|---|---|
| Brewing method: | C; Single infusion mash, top fermented | | |
| Mash liquor: | 11 litres | Alcohol content: | 4.1% |
| Mash temperature: | 65°C | Final gravity: | 1010 |
| Mash time: | 90 minutes | Bitterness: | 28 EBU |
| Boil time: | 2 hours | Final volume: | 23 litres |

# Woodforde's PHOENIX XXX

A strong, mellow and complex ale from Woodforde's Norfolk brewery.
Rounded malt in the mouth, deep, "fruity" finish with pear drop character.

Classification:   English Cask-Conditioned Bitter

Original gravity:           1047

*In the mash tun*

| | | |
|---|---|---|
| Pale malt: | 4,800 g | (90%) |
| Crystal malt: | 530 g | (10%) |

*In the copper*

| | | |
|---|---|---|
| Goldings hops: | 60 g | (start of boil) |
| Goldings hops: | 12 g | (last 15 minutes) |
| Irish moss: | 1 tsp | (last 15 minutes) |

*Typical characteristics*

| | | | |
|---|---|---|---|
| Brewing method: | C; Single infusion mash, top fermented | | |
| Mash liquor: | 13 litres | Alcohol content: | 4.8% |
| Mash temperature: | 66°C | Final gravity: | 1011 |
| Mash time: | 90 minutes | Bitterness: | 22 EBU |
| Boil time: | 2 hours | Final volume: | 23 litres |

MALT EXTRACT VERSION – No mash required

Replace the pale malt with 3,500 grams of non-diastatic, medium coloured
malt extract.  Brew using Malt Extract Brewing – Method A.

# Youngs SPECIAL BITTER

A beautifully crafted premium bitter from Youngs Wandsworth brewery. Rounded malt with good hop underpinning. Deep bitter sweet finish.

Classification:   English Cask-Conditioned Pale Ale

Original gravity:          1046

*In the mash tun*

| | | |
|---|---|---|
| Pale malt: | 4,700 g | (92%) |
| Torrefied barley: | 150 g | (3%) |
| Chocolate malt: | 50 g | (1%) |

*In the copper*

| | | |
|---|---|---|
| Maltose syrup: | 200 g | (4%) |
| Fuggles hops: | 38 g | (start of boil) |
| Goldings hops: | 32 g | (start of boil) |
| Irish moss: | 1 tsp | (last 15 minutes) |
| Goldings hops: | 4 g | (start of boil) |

*Typical characteristics*

| | | | |
|---|---|---|---|
| Brewing method: | C; Single infusion mash, top fermented | | |
| Mash liquor: | 12 litres | Alcohol content: | 4.7% |
| Mash temperature: | 66°C | Final gravity: | 1011 |
| Mash time: | 90 minutes | Bitterness: | 32 EBU |
| Boil time: | 2 hours | Final volume: | 23 litres |

# 13 Porter & Stout Recipes

*All of the London Porter is professed to be "entire butt", as indeed it was at first, but the system is now altered and it is very generally compounded of two kinds, or rather the same liquor in two different stages, the due admixture of which is palatable though neither is good alone. One is mild, the other is stale Porter; the former is that which has a slightly bitter flavour from having lately been brewed; the latter has been kept longer. This mixture the publican adapts to the palates of his several customers and affects the mixture very readily by means of a machine containing small pumps worked by a handle.*

*- Rees Cyclopedia, 1819-20*

## Porter (entire)

This particularly enigmatic drink was the favourite of Londoners for more than 150 years. It originates from the early eighteenth century when the Londoners of that period had the habit of drinking a mixture of beers in much the same way as modern drinkers mix mild and bitter. Obadiah Poundage, writing in 1760, said: "Some drank mild beer and stale mixed; others ale, mild beer and stale blended together at threepence per quart; but many used all stale at fourpence per pot [quart]."

The term *mild* meant freshly brewed immature beer; not quite the same as the modern meaning. The *stale* beer was a deliberate ingredient to enhance the flavour and was not spoiled beer being flogged off cheaply, as some commentators have suggested. Stale was another word for matured and such ales were twice the price of the mild (fresh) ales. Stales had been kept for a year or more and had turned sour, providing an acetic flavour much relished by Londoners. The drinker mixed mild and stale in his tankard in appropriate quantities to give him his preferred degree of acidic tang.

Popular ale lore has it that in 1722 Ralph Harwood of the Bell Brewhouse at Shoreditch brewed a new drink to match the qualities of the mixtures, but which could be drawn from one cask rather than two or three. It is said that the new drink took London by storm, and within a few years it had become the universal drink among the working classes of London. It is also said that Ralph Harwood first called the new drink *Entire Butt*, but it came to be known as *Porter* in London, apparently due to its popularity with the Porters of the London markets.

The real secret of the original London "entire" was that it was *deliberately* soured; a fact which few writers and historians seem to have realised. The genuine London "entire" of old was a blend of freshly-brewed brown beer and moderately aged brown beer, to which was added a quantity of sour beer before leaving the brewery. This provided the acidic after-tang that Londoners relished so greatly. Another point is that Porter, or entire, was not originally black in colour as many people suppose; but a murky brown.

The London brewers built huge storage vats in which to age their Porter; aged Porter took over a year to mature. The oxidation of alcohol into acetic acid is a very slow process, and took a long time to complete. The London Porter brewers were very proud of their maturation vats and were in the habit of forever building bigger ones. Million-gallon vats were not uncommon; parties and dances were often held in them as opening ceremonies. In 1814 one of these vats, containing three quarters of a million gallons of Porter, burst and demolished part of Richard Meux's brewery and a row of terraced cottages, killing eight people in the process. Fortunately it was one of their smaller vats!

From that point onwards the brewers were less ambitious regarding the size of their Porter vats. Breweries had a very disagreeable habit of catching fire and burning down. This happened to the Barclay Perkins brewery in 1832, despite the fact that: *"The contents of the great beer vats, containing several thousand barrels of beer, were poured out to supply the engines."* The same newspaper report also makes reference to the fact that the scene was *"flanked by a powerful body of police, forming an outpost of defence"* and to *"the intemperate precipitation of the strangers who tendered their services"*. No doubt buckshee Porter was running along the gutters! I remember a similar incident when a Guinness road-tanker overturned near High Wycombe many years ago.

It would be difficult, if not controversial, to try to define a traditional Porter or Entire. Not only were the Porter brewers of London very secretive about their methods, but the phenomenal success of Porter caused almost every brewer to attempt to jump on the bandwagon with his own look-alike and taste-alike version. Add to this the fact that Porter's heyday lasted for well over 150 years, and it becomes plain that the drink had more than enough time in which to evolve and change considerably. There is also no doubt that London Porter was quite different from provincial Porter; as James Herbert points out in The Art of Brewing, 1871: *"There is such a disparity between the London Porter and the Provincial brewed Porter, that I am almost at a loss of which to treat on."*

The original London Porters were simply brown ales that were deliberately soured. In those days colour was synonymous with strength. Porter was progressively weakened to maintain its price in the face of ever rising malt tax, and progressively darkened to give the impression of higher strength. Porter then became to be made from high-dried brown malt and black strap (molasses). Additional colour and a burnt bitter taste was provided by boiling molasses until it was dark, bitter, and thick, and then it was set on fire and burned for a few minutes. Molasses, apart from being much cheaper than malt, probably fell outside of the scope of the malt tax and was therefore duty free. The use of sugar was illegal, but molasses probably fooled the authorities for a while. This will help to explain why Porter was quite a cheap drink, and why the brewers kept their recipes a closely guarded secret – in case the excise men caught onto the fiddle! By the end of that century the standard grist for Porter had become equal parts of amber and brown malts. The burnt taste was supplied by actually setting fire to a portion of the brown malt and charring it. By the early 1800s the standard grist

140

had become a mixture of amber, brown, pale, and black malts, the burnt taste being supplied by the black malt.

Pale malt was kilned over a coal fire, but brown malts were kilned over hardwood fires, usually hornbeam. The kilning of the malts over hardwood fires gave the malts a characteristic smoky flavour similar to whisky malts. The smoky flavour would have been one of the major characteristics of Porter, and indeed of any beer of the period except pale ale.

Bottled Guinness and Courage Russian Imperial Stout both began life as Porters, although they are quite different style beers. Both could probably be considered representative of the changes that have taken place in Porter brewing over the years. The ingredients of Russian Stout resemble the late London Porters very closely, but the brewing techniques of Guinness are more appropriate to early Porters. Both have, no doubt, changed considerably over the years.

A number of modern breweries make a drink which they call Porter, but none of them brews the real thing; all three distinguishing characteristics are missing. A true London Porter would have a smoky flavour provided by the brown malts, a burnt bitter taste contributed by the black malt and an acetic tang provided by the deliberate souring. These facts coupled with a much higher hop rate, and the fact that London Porters were not originally black in colour, but a transparent dark brown means that modern Porters are nothing like the genuine thing, but then I would be surprised if a real Porter, made as it was 150 years ago, would find favour with the modern palate.

## Stout

Stout began life as a stronger version of Porter. In the old days, before sparging was introduced, a brewer would mash a given batch of grain three times. This would give three worts, or gyles, of successively lower gravity. The London brewers tended to combine all three gyles into one beer and this produced the standard London Porters of about OG 1070, but if the three gyles were made into separate brews rather than being combined, they would produce three beers of different strengths. The stout would come off the first mash at OG 1110, best Porter from the second at OG 1085, and table beer from the third at about OG 1050. Country brewers usually brewed the three gyles separately, whereas London brewers combined the gyles and this would account for the disparity in strength between London and provincial Porters. One old reference states that:

> "The Porter brewed in London, usually sold at threepence and fourpence per pot (quart), would not suit the public in the country; they prefer paying sixpence, and have it heavier than London Brewed beer."

Stout has changed over the years, and has, with a couple of exceptions, moved quite a long way from its origins. The notion that stout was full of goodness encouraged the practice of prescribing stout for medicinal purposes, and this in turn brought about a trend in sweet "food stouts" which became very popular because of their supposed nutritional benefit. Invalid Stout, Tonic Stout, Oatmeal Stout, Oyster Stout, Butter Stout, Milk Stout and Sweet Stout are the most common examples, but they have nearly all disappeared now.

**Fermentation can produce a lively yeast head**

# Beamish IRISH STOUT

A dark Irish stout, from the Beamish & Crawford brewery in Cork. Roast barley, chocolate and hops in the mouth, bitter finish with some fruit and hop notes and slight astringency.

Classification:   Irish Stout (sold commercially in keg form)

Original gravity:          1039

*In the mash tun*

| | | |
|---|---|---|
| Pale malt: | 2,800 g | (66%) |
| Chocolate malt: | 170 g | (4%) |
| Roasted barley: | 420 g | (10%) |
| Wheat malt: | 420 g | (10%) |

*In the copper*

| | | |
|---|---|---|
| Cane sugar: | 210 g | (5%) |
| Maltose syrup: | 210 g | (5%) |
| Northdown hops: | 31 g | (start of boil) |
| Styrian Golding hops: | 35 g | (start of boil) |
| Styrian Golding hops: | 15 g | (last 15 minutes) |

*Typical characteristics*

| | | | |
|---|---|---|---|
| Brewing method: | C ; Single infusion mash, top fermented. | | |
| Mash liquor: | 10 litres | Alcohol content: | 4.1% |
| Mash temperature: | 66°C | Final gravity: | 1009 |
| Mash time: | 2 hours | Bitterness: | 40 EBU |
| Boil time: | 2 hours | Final volume: | 23 litres |

MALT EXTRACT VERSION – Partial mash required

Replace the pale malt with 2,000 grams of diastatic malt extract such as EDME DMS. Brew using Malt Extract Brewing – Method B.

# Caledonian PORTER

A dark, delectable brew from the Caledonian brewery in Edinburgh. Biscuity in the mouth, dry finish with good hop character.

Classification:   Scottish Cask-Conditioned Beer.

Original gravity:          1042

*In the mash tun*

| | | |
|---|---|---|
| Pale malt: | 3,300 g | (68%) |
| Crystal malt: | 340 g | (7%) |
| Amber malt: | 480 g | (10%) |
| Chocolate malt: | 290 g | (6%) |
| Black malt: | 190 g | (4%) |
| Wheat malt: | 240 g | (5%) |

*In the copper*

| | | |
|---|---|---|
| Fuggles hops: | 48 g | (start of boil) |
| Goldings hops: | 41 g | (start of boil) |
| Goldings hops: | 25 g | (last 15 minutes) |

*Typical characteristics*

| | | | |
|---|---|---|---|
| Brewing method: | C; Single infusion mash, top fermented. | | |
| Mash liquor: | 12 litres | Alcohol content: | 4.0% |
| Mash temperature: | 66°C | Final gravity: | 1012 |
| Mash time: | 2 hours | Bitterness: | 35 EBU |
| Boil time: | 2 hours | Final volume: | 23 litres |

# Courage IMPERIAL RUSSIAN STOUT

This beer has its origins rooted firmly in the London Porter tradition. It was first brewed by Barclay Perkins and became a firm favourite with the Russian court. It used to be known as "Russian Imperial Stout" until the Imperial Tobacco Group took over Courage. It is now brewed at the John Smith's brewery in Tadcaster. Stunningly dry, bitter black chocolate on tongue with deep, intense finish, great hop bitterness, and rich dark fruit.

Classification:    Bottle-Conditioned Stout Porter.

Original gravity:             1104

*In the mash tun*

| | | |
|---|---|---|
| Pale malt: | 5,350 g | (50%) |
| Amber malt: | 1,600 g | (15%) |
| Black malt: | 540 g | (5%) |

*In the copper*

| | | |
|---|---|---|
| Malt extract: | 1,950 g | (18%) |
| Maltose syrup: | 1,300 g | (12%) |
| Goldings hops: | 82 g | (start of boil) |
| Fuggles hops: | 97 g | (start of boil) |
| Fuggles hops: | 36 g | (last 15 minutes) |

*Typical characteristics*

| | | | |
|---|---|---|---|
| Brewing method: | C; Single infusion mash, top fermented. | | |
| Mash liquor | 18 litres | Alcohol content: | 10.2% |
| Mash temperature: | 67°C | Final gravity: | 1028 |
| Mash time: | 2 hours | Bitterness: | 70 EBU |
| Boil time: | 2 hours | Final volume: | 23 litres |

## NOTES

The great old grandad of British beers. If the amber malt is not available, replace with pale malt. Pitch with a high quality ale yeast, but have a wine yeast or a reviver yeast handy to re-pitch if fermentation should get stuck, but use only in an emergency. Observe that the final gravity is quite high. Barrel the beer after fermentation and mature for a year or more. Then bottle and mature for at least a further year. Reputedly at its best after three years!

# Edwin Taylor's EXTRA STOUT

A superb stout from Banks & Taylor's Shefford brewery. Ripe malt with strong roast notes. Rich deep finish with rich balance of hops, bitter malt and chocolate.

Classification:   Cask-Conditioned English Stout

Original gravity:          1042

*In the mash tun*

| | | |
|---|---|---|
| Pale malt: | 4,000 g | (84%) |
| Roast barley: | 770 g | (16%) |

*In the copper*

| | | |
|---|---|---|
| Challenger hops: | 39 g | (start of boil) |
| Hallertau hops: | 40 g | (start of boil) |

*Typical characteristics*

| | | | |
|---|---|---|---|
| Brewing method: | C; Single infusion mash, top fermented. | | |
| Mash liquor | 12 litres | Alcohol content: | 4.2% |
| Mash temperature: | 67°C | Final gravity: | 1011 |
| Mash time: | 2 hours | Bitterness: | 48 EBU |
| Boil time: | 2 hours | Final volume: | 23 litres |

MALT EXTRACT VERSION – No mash required

Replace the pale malt with 2,950 grams of non-diastatic, medium- coloured malt extract. Brew using Malt Extract Brewing – Method A.

# Guinness EXTRA STOUT

A world classic beer of enormous complexity and character.

Classification:     Dry Irish Stout.

Original gravity:          1042

*In the mash tun*

| | | |
|---|---|---|
| Pale malt: | 3,900 g | (80%) |
| Roast barley: | 490 g | (10%) |
| Flaked barley | 490 g | (10%) |

*In the copper*

| | | |
|---|---|---|
| Challenger hops: | 37 g | (start of boil) |
| Target hops: | 25 g | (start of boil) |

*Typical characteristics*

| | | | |
|---|---|---|---|
| Brewing method: | C; Single infusion mash, top fermented. | | |
| Mash liquor | 12 litres | Alcohol content: | 4.2% |
| Mash temperature: | 66°C | Final gravity: | 1010 |
| Mash time: | 2 hours | Bitterness: | 45 EBU |
| Boil time: | 2 hours | Final volume: | 23 litres |

## NOTES

A single temperature infusion mash can be used in this recipe, as has been the case for the odd century or two. These days Guinness have a high tech brew house, and use a temperature-programmed mash.

MALT EXTRACT VERSION – Partial mash required

Replace the pale malt with 2,800 grams of diastatic malt extract such as EDME DMS. Brew using Malt Extract Brewing – Method B.

# Linfit ENGLISH GUINEAS STOUT

A tasty, dark stout from the Linfit brewery in Huddersfield. Rich nut and hop prickle on tongue, dry chocolate finish.

Classification:      English Stout

Original gravity:      1050

*In the mash tun*

| | | |
|---|---|---|
| Pale malt: | 4,950 g | (87%) |
| Roasted barley | 680 g | (12%) |
| Flaked barley: | 55 g | (1%) |

*In the copper*

| | | |
|---|---|---|
| Challenger hops: | 71 g | (start of boil) |
| Challenger hops: | 20 g | (last 15 minutes) |

*Typical characteristics*

| | | | |
|---|---|---|---|
| Brewing method: | C; Single infusion mash, top fermented. | | |
| Mash liquor: | 14 litres | Alcohol content: | 5.0% |
| Mash temperature: | 66°C | Final gravity: | 1013 |
| Mash time: | 2 hours | Bitterness: | 44 EBU |
| Boil time: | 2 hours | Final volume: | 23 litres |

MALT EXTRACT VERSION – Partial mash required

Replace the pale malt with 3,650 grams of diastatic malt extract such as EDME DMS. Brew using Malt Extract Brewing – Method B.

# 14 Old Ale, Stock Ale and Barley Wine

*Some persons do not relish Ale until it becomes old. In making a recently brewed Ale drink old the publican will find no difficulty, as it is very easy to be accomplished, provided that he has a barrel or two of sour Beer; add two gallons of the latter, with a pound and a half of the best Hops well rubbed, and one pound of sugar candy dissolved in the Beer.*

*– The Art of Brewing, James Herbert, 1871*

It took some deliberation to decide what the contents of this section should be. The problem is that although a number of breweries produce a beer which they call Old Ale, or Stock Ale, very few of them brew the real thing in the traditional sense. Far too often Old Ales are nothing other than the brewery's bog-standard 1040 to 1045 bitter which has been darkened by adulterating it with caramel. There is nothing whatsoever old about such an ale, and it should not be termed such. It is not strong, it is not brewed to an old recipe, it is not brewed using old methods, and it certainly has not been matured for any length of time.

The acrid taste of high levels of caramel and the dark colour give the mouth-feel and appearance of strength, and one is accordingly charged 20-30 per cent more for it. This sort of practice I consider to be a gross misrepresentation of a product type, and the sort of thing that would cause consumer uproar if it happened in almost any other industry.

Old ales seem to have been with us for ever. In the early days of commercial brewing it was customary for the publican to send his own casks to the brewery to be filled, and it was the publican's responsibility to mature the ale. The strong ales of the day took a long time to mature, so this was an expensive commitment for the humble publican. Obviously old matured ale was considerably more expensive than mild (new) ale because it needed to be stored for a year or more.

Modern old ales are related to stock ales, which have an independent history. In the old days of brewing it was not possible to brew good, sound ales during the summer months because of problems with infection. It was common practice to brew the whole summer's supply of ale during the winter brewing season, which ran from about October to May, and store it until summer. Eventually it was learned that some brewing could take place during the summer if freshly brewed beer was blended with strong, sound and fully matured ale.

The qualities of the matured ale apparently improved the new beer to the extent that little maturation time was required and the ale could be sent out of the brewery almost immediately, with the result that it was drunk before it had a chance to go off. This blending technique was known as "hardening", or "bringing forward", and Brakspear of Henley among others practised it.

By this technique a very strong "stock ale" was brewed during the winter and put into store. This was used for blending purposes during the following summer, and any surplus left over by the time the next winter's brewing season came around was sent out to the pubs as "old ale". This ale was a very high-quality, potent old nectar which had been matured for nearly a year, and it was probably eagerly lapped up by a grateful public. However, it could only remain on sale until the supply ran out, and this probably accounts for the modern tradition of breweries supplying a limited-edition strong winter brew.

It is not clear, to me at least, how the blending process improved fresh ale. The quantities of old ale blended with the fresh were, apparently, quite small. The old ale would have developed an acidic character during maturation and I suspect that it is this quality that showed through in the final ale. The use of a high proportion of acidic, black malts would also assist in this direction. The use of black malts may account for the modern custom of making old ales appear very dark in colour.

The original stock ales, or "Keeping Ales", were brewed using special techniques. They were mashed at high temperatures which produced a dextrinous wort, they were boiled for extended periods, and they were heavily hopped. Their gravity was around 1110, and they were matured for up to a year before being blended or sold as old ale.

I suppose that technically a modern "old ale" should be an ale that has been matured for an extended period of time, but for this to make sense it must be an ale of a quality and strength that will benefit considerably from a long maturation period. As very few breweries do such things, the criterion for selection of beers in this section are those ales which have an OG of around 1060 or more, and have something special about them. They include Old Ales, Stock Ales, Winter Specials, and Barley Wines; Porters and Stouts have their own section.

Barley wine is a modern, euphemistic term for a very strong ale. At one time all ales were at this sort of strength and were simply called "ale". I suppose a barley wine should have an OG of at least 1090, to be worthy of the term.

# Banks & Taylor BLACK BAT

A dangerously potent and complex beer from the Banks & Taylor brewery in Shefford, Bedfordshire. Vast, fruity, malt and hop flavours, deep, bitter sweet finish with delicious balance of hops and nutty malt.

Classification:   English Cask-Conditioned Ale

Original gravity:         1064

*In the mash tun*

| | | |
|---|---|---|
| Pale malt: | 6,500 g | (89%) |
| Crystal malt: | 730 g | (10%) |
| Black malt: | 72 g | (1%) |

*In the copper*

| | | |
|---|---|---|
| Challenger hops: | 34 g | (start of boil) |
| Fuggles hops: | 58 g | (start of boil) |
| Goldings hops: | 20 g | (last 15 minutes) |

*Typical characteristics*

| | | | |
|---|---|---|---|
| Brewing method: | C; Single infusion mash, top fermented. | | |
| Mash liquor: | 17 litres | Alcohol content: | 6.5% |
| Mash temperature: | 67°C | Final gravity: | 1015 |
| Mash time: | 2 hours | Bitterness: | 42 EBU |
| Boil time: | 2 hours | Final volume: | 23 litres |

MALT EXTRACT VERSION – No mash required

Replace the pale malt with 4,750 grams of non-diastatic, medium- coloured malt extract. Brew using Malt Extract Brewing – Method A.

# Bateman's WINTER WARMER

A rounded strong ale with complex aromas and flavours from George Bateman's Wainfleet brewery. Sweet, nutty malt in the mouth, dry biscuit and hops finish.

Classification:   Cask-Conditioned Winter Brew

Original gravity:          1058

*In the mash tun*

| | | |
|---|---|---|
| Pale malt: | 4,000 g | (66%) |
| Black malt: | 180 g | (3%) |
| Roast barley: | 400 g | (6.5%) |
| Flaked wheat: | 280 g | (4.5%) |

*In the copper*

| | | |
|---|---|---|
| Invert cane sugar: | 1,200 g | (20%) |
| Goldings hops: | 95 g | (start of boil) |
| Goldings hops: | 20 g | (last 15 minutes) |

*Typical characteristics*

| | | | |
|---|---|---|---|
| Brewing method: | C; Single infusion mash, top fermented | | |
| Mash liquor: | 12 litres | Alcohol content: | 6.7% |
| Mash temperature: | 67°C | Final gravity: | 1008 |
| Mash time: | 2 hours | Bitterness: | 40 EBU |
| Boil time: | 2 hours | Final volume: | 23 litres |

MALT EXTRACT VERSION – Partial mash required

Replace the pale malt with 2,900 grams of diastatic malt extract such as EDME DMS. Brew using Malt Extract Brewing – Method B.

# Big Lamp OLD GENIE

A sumptuous, strong and complex dark beer from the Big Lamp Brewery in Newcastle. Heavy, mouth filling malt; vast bitter-sweet finish with complex banana and gooseberry notes.

Classification:   English Cask-Conditioned Bitter

Original gravity:          1068

*In the mash tun*

| | | |
|---|---|---|
| Pale malt: | 5,800 g | (78%) |
| Crystal malt: | 670 g | (9%) |
| Black Malt: | 220 g | (3%) |

*In the copper*

| | | |
|---|---|---|
| Invert cane sugar: | 740 g | (10%) |
| Fuggles hops: | 73 g | (start of boil) |
| Goldings hops: | 41 g | (start of boil) |
| Goldings hops: | 15 g | (last 15 minutes) |
| Fuggles hops: | 5 g | (dry hops in cask) |

*Typical characteristics*

| | | | |
|---|---|---|---|
| Brewing method: | C; Single infusion mash, top fermented. | | |
| Mash liquor: | 16 litres | Alcohol content: | 7.4% |
| Mash temperature: | 67°C | Final gravity: | 1013 |
| Mash time: | 2 hours | Bitterness: | 44 EBU |
| Boil time: | 2 hours | Final volume: | 23 litres |

MALT EXTRACT VERSION – No mash required

Replace the pale malt with 4,200 grams of non-diastatic, medium coloured malt extract. Brew using Malt Extract Brewing – Method A.

# Broughton OLD JOCK

A rich and satisfying ale, good for drinking on its own or through a meal. Full tasting malt and hop in the mouth; deep bitter sweet finish with hints of vanilla.

Classification:   Cask-Conditioned Strong Ale

Original gravity:          1070

*In the mash tun*

| | | |
|---|---|---|
| Pale malt: | 6,000 g | (80%) |
| Roast barley: | 450 g | (6%) |

*In the copper*

| | | |
|---|---|---|
| Maltose syrup: | 1000 g | (14%) |
| Fuggles hops: | 65 g | (start of boil) |
| Goldings hops: | 55 g | (start of boil) |
| Goldings hops: | 5 g | (dry hops in cask) |

*Typical characteristics*

Brewing method:        C; Single infusion mash, top fermented.

| | | | |
|---|---|---|---|
| Mash liquor: | 18 litres | Alcohol content: | 7.4% |
| Mash temperature: | 67°C | Final gravity: | 1015 |
| Mash time: | 2 hours | Bitterness: | 46 EBU |
| Boil time: | 2 hours | Final volume: | 23 litres |

MALT EXTRACT VERSION – No mash required

Replace the pale malt with 4,400 grams of non-diastatic, medium coloured malt extract. Brew using Malt Extract Brewing – Method A.

# Crouch Vale WILLIE WARMER

A powerful, sipping strong ale from the Crouch Vale brewery in Essex. Roast barley and ripe fruit in the mouth; rich bitter-sweet finish with hints of fruit and nut.

Classification:   English Cask-Conditioned Winter Brew

Original gravity:          1060

*In the mash tun*

| | | |
|---|---|---|
| Pale malt: | 6,150 g | (90%) |
| Crystal malt: | 340 g | (5%) |
| Roast barley: | 340 g | (5%) |

*In the copper*

| | | |
|---|---|---|
| Challenger hops: | 65 g | (start of boil) |
| Challenger hops: | 15 g | (last 15 minutes) |

*Typical characteristics*

| | | | |
|---|---|---|---|
| Brewing method: | C; Single infusion mash, top fermented. | | |
| Mash liquor: | 16 litres | Alcohol content: | 6.1% |
| Mash temperature: | 67°C | Final gravity: | 1014 |
| Mash time: | 2 hours | Bitterness: | 40 EBU |
| Boil time: | 2 hours | Final volume: | 23 litres |

MALT EXTRACT VERSION – No mash required

Replace the pale malt with 4,500 grams of non-diastatic, medium coloured malt extract. Brew using Malt Extract Brewing – Method A.

# Eldridge Pope THOMAS HARDY'S ALE

It is customary to quote from Thomas Hardy's Mayor of Casterbridge when writing about this particular beer: "Full in body; piquant, yet without a twang; free from streakiness." Thomas Hardy's Ale was first brewed in 1968 to mark the fortieth anniversary of the novelist's death. My feeling is that Eldridge Pope could not have liked him very much if they celebrate his death! This is the strongest ale regularly brewed in England, and it is a high quality, all malt brew to boot.

Classification:   English Bottle-Conditioned Strong Ale

Original gravity:          1125

*In the mash tun*

| Pale malt:\ | 6,800 g | (80%) |
| Amber malt: | 1,700 g | (20%) |

*In the copper*

| Golding hops: | 55 g | (start of boil) |
| Fuggles hops: | 65 g | (start of boil) |
| Styrian Goldings: | 25 g | (last 15 minutes) |
| Irish moss: | 2 tsp | (last 15 minutes) |

*Typical characteristics*

| Brewing method: | C; Single infusion mash, top fermented. | | |
| Mash liquor: | 18 litres | Alcohol content: | 12.8% |
| Mash temperature: | 67°C | Final gravity: | 1030 |
| Mash time: | 2 hours | Bitterness: | 75 EBU |
| Boil time: | 1½ – 2½ hours | Final volume: | 12 litres |

OBSERVE THAT THIS RECIPE MAKES ONLY 12 LITRES (2½ GALLONS).

For instructions see next page.

## Brewing notes for Thomas Hardy's Ale:

Our vessels are not big enough to brew efficiently 23 litres of an OG 1125 ale. The obvious answer to the problem is to brew a smaller batch. Home-brew shops sell 2½ gallon (12 litre) barrels, and this volume is just about as much as we can achieve at such strength.

You will need two types of yeast, a 2½ gallon barrel for maturation, and 60 nip bottles or 40 half-pint bottles. If you cannot get the amber malt, replace it with pale malt.

Mash and sparge as a normal beer, but stop sparging when you have collected about 15 litres (3 gallons) of wort.

Boil for a minimum of 1½ hours but long enough to reduce the volume to 12 litres (2½ gallons) or less.

Cool the wort and then adjust to OG 1125 with water in the fermentation vessel. You should have about 12 litres (2½ gallons) of wort.

Aerate the wort and pitch with a high quality English Ale yeast.

Monitor SG carefully and if the fermentation gets stuck, i.e. stops before about SG 1035, rack the beer off the yeast, into another fermentation vessel, and re-pitch with a wine yeast. If a wine yeast is used then fit the lid and an airlock to the vessel.

When fermentation has abated, rack the beer off the yeast into a 2½ gallon (12 litre) barrel and add a sachet of wine yeast to the barrel. Fit the cap, put the barrel away somewhere and forget about it for three months.

After three months recover the barrel, and rack into a sterilised fermentation vessel on to 50 grams of sugar and a 5 gram sachet of wine yeast. Ensure that the wine yeast, sugar and beer get well mixed, but try to ensure that a minimum of air gets dissolved into the beer.

Bottle the beer, and cap. Store for a minimum of one year. Reputedly best at five years.

# Everards OLD BILL

A fruity strong ale, brewed by Everard's from October to January. Rich balance of sweet malt and hops with dry fruit finish.

Classification:   English Cask-Conditioned Ale

Original gravity:          1070

*In the mash tun*

| | | |
|---|---|---|
| Pale malt: | 5,250 g | (65%) |
| Crystal malt: | 790 g | (11%) |

*In the copper*

| | | |
|---|---|---|
| Invert sugar: | 290 g | (4%) |
| Maltose syrup: | 1,450 g | (20%) |
| Challenger hops: | 32 g | (start of boil) |
| Fuggles hops: | 36 g | (start of boil) |
| Goldings hops: | 18 g | (last 15 minutes) |

*Typical characteristics*

| | | | |
|---|---|---|---|
| Brewing method: | C; Single infusion mash, top fermented | | |
| Mash liquor: | 14 litres | Alcohol content: | 7.4% |
| Mash temperature: | 66°C | Final gravity: | 1015 |
| Mash time: | 2 hours | Bitterness: | 33 EBU |
| Boil time: | 2 hours | Final volume: | 23 litres |

NOTE
Everards actually use caramel for colouring in their beers.

MALT EXTRACT VERSION – No mash required

Replace the pale malt with 3,800 grams of non-diastatic, medium coloured malt extract. Brew using Malt Extract Brewing – Method A.

# Gale's PRIZE OLD ALE

A superb, deep, red barley wine supplied in corked bottles. Great, mouth filling malt and fruit in the mouth, intensely dry finish with raisin hints.

Classification:   English Bottle-Conditioned Barley Wine

Original gravity:          1094

*In the mash tun*

| | | |
|---|---|---|
| Pale malt: | 7,000 g | (70%) |
| Black malt: | 50 g | (0.5%) |
| Wheat flour: | 145 g | (1.5%) |

*In the copper*

| | | |
|---|---|---|
| Malt extract: | 2,450 g | (11%) |
| Goldings hops: | 33 g | (start of boil) |
| Fuggles hops: | 95 g | (start of boil) |
| Goldings hops: | 40 g | (last 15 minutes) |

*Typical characteristics*

| | | | |
|---|---|---|---|
| Brewing method: | C; Single infusion mash, top fermented | | |
| Mash liquor: | 17 litres | Alcohol content: | 9.6% |
| Mash temperature: | 66°C | Final gravity: | 1023 |
| Mash time: | 2 hours | Bitterness: | 48 EBU |
| Boil time: | 2 hours | Final volume: | 23 litres |

## NOTES

The malt extract is included because it is difficult to mash a high volume of grain efficiently in our home-brew equipment. Any light coloured, non-diastatic liquid malt extract can be used.

# Holden's OLD ALE

A dark and dangerously potable winter brew from Holden's Woodsetton brewery in the West Midlands. Malty in the mouth with roast notes; long, deep finish with hop, dark chocolate and raisins.

Classification:   English Cask-Conditioned Winter Warmer

Original gravity:          1092

*In the mash tun*

| | | |
|---|---|---|
| Pale malt: | 6,100 g | (65%) |
| Black malt: | 190 g | (2%) |
| Roast barley: | 470 g | (5%) |

*In the copper*

| | | |
|---|---|---|
| Malt extract: | 1,700 g | (18%) |
| Invert cane sugar: | 940 g | (10%) |
| Fuggles hops: | 70 g | (start of boil) |
| Goldings hops: | 40 g | (start of boil) |
| Goldings hops: | 30 g | (last 15 minutes) |

*Typical characteristics*

| | | | |
|---|---|---|---|
| Brewing method: | C; Single infusion mash, top fermented | | |
| Mash liquor: | 17 litres | Alcohol content: | 9.9% |
| Mash temperature: | 67°C | Final gravity: | 1018 |
| Mash time: | 2 hours | Bitterness: | 42 EBU |
| Boil time: | 2 hours | Final volume: | 23 litres |

## NOTES

The malt extract is included because it is difficult to mash a high volume of grain efficiently in our home-brew equipment. Any light coloured, non-diastatic liquid malt extract can be used.

# Hoskins & Oldfield OLD NAVIGATION

A powerful and complex old ale from this Leicester brewery. Massive and complex bitter sweet fruit flavours in mouth; long, vinous finish with sweet fruit dominating.

Classification:   English Cask-Conditioned Old Ale

Original gravity:              1071

*In the mash tun*

| | | |
|---|---|---|
| Pale malt: | 6,200 g | (80%) |
| Crystal malt: | 780 g | (10%) |

*In the copper*

| | | |
|---|---|---|
| Invert cane sugar: | 780 g | (10%) |
| Goldings hops: | 95 g | (start of boil) |
| Goldings hops: | 20 g | (last 15 minutes) |

*Typical characteristics*

| | | | |
|---|---|---|---|
| Brewing method: | C; Single infusion mash, top fermented | | |
| Mash liquor: | 17 litres | Alcohol content: | 7.9% |
| Mash temperature: | 67°C | Final gravity: | 1013 |
| Mash time: | 2 hours | Bitterness: | 38 EBU |
| Boil time: | 2 hours | Final volume: | 23 litres |

MALT EXTRACT VERSION – No mash required

Replace the pale malt with 4,550 grams of non-diastatic, light- coloured malt extract. Brew using Malt Extract Brewing – Method A.

# Linfit ENOCH'S HAMMER

A straw coloured beer for sipping, a rich and powerful brew from this Huddersfield brewery. Vast, shattering attack of malt, orange and lemon peel with memorably long finish of hoppy dryness and fruity astringency.

Classification:   English Cask-Conditioned Strong Ale

Original gravity:          1080

*In the mash tun*

| | | |
|---|---|---|
| Pale malt: | 6,750 g | (80%) |
| Flaked barley: | 85 g | (1%) |

*In the copper*

| | | |
|---|---|---|
| Malt extract: | 1,600 g | (19%) |
| Goldings hops: | 85 g | (start of boil) |
| Goldings hops: | 20 g | (last 15 minutes) |

*Typical characteristics*

| | | | |
|---|---|---|---|
| Brewing method: | C; Single infusion mash, top fermented | | |
| Mash liquor: | 17 litres | Alcohol content: | 8.2% |
| Mash temperature: | 67°C | Final gravity: | 1019 |
| Mash time: | 2 hours | Bitterness: | 35 EBU |
| Boil time: | 2 hours | Final volume: | 23 litres |

## NOTES

The malt extract is included because it is difficult to mash a high volume of grain efficiently in our home-brew equipment. Any light coloured, non-diastatic liquid malt extract can be used.

# Morland's OLD SPECKLED HEN

A richly coloured and flavoured strong ale with generous hop character from the Morland's Abingdon brewery. First brewed to commemorate the fiftieth anniversary of the MG car factory in Abingdon. Old Speckled Hen was the affectionate name for an early MG model, so named because of the speckled pattern of its paintwork.

Classification:   English Cask-Conditioned Ale

Original gravity:        1050

*In the mash tun*

| | | |
|---|---|---|
| Pale malt: | 4,350 g | (80%) |
| Crystal malt: | 540 g | (10%) |

*In the copper*

| | | |
|---|---|---|
| Invert cane sugar: | 540 g | (10%) |
| Challenger hops: | 65 g | (start of boil) |
| Goldings hops: | 15 g | (last 15 minutes) |
| Irish moss: | 1 tsp | (last 15 minutes) |
| Goldings hops: | 5 g | (dry hopped in cask) |

*Typical characteristics*

| | | | |
|---|---|---|---|
| Brewing method: | C; Single infusion mash, top fermented | | |
| Mash liquor: | 12 litres | Alcohol content: | 5.6% |
| Mash temperature: | 66°C | Final gravity: | 1009 |
| Mash time: | 2 hours | Bitterness: | 40 EBU |
| Boil time: | 2 hours | Final volume: | 23 litres |

MALT EXTRACT VERSION – No mash required

Replace the pale malt with 3,150 grams of non-diastatic, light coloured malt extract. Brew using Malt Extract Brewing – Method A.

# Nethergate OLD GROWLER

A dark and smooth ale from the Nethergate brewery in Sudbury, Suffolk. Full and bitter sweet in mouth with deep finish and hints of dark chocolate.

Classification:   English Cask-Conditioned Old Ale

Original gravity:          1055

*In the mash tun*

| | | |
|---|---|---|
| Pale malt: | 5,300 g | (85%) |
| Crystal malt: | 530 g | (8.5%) |
| Black malt: | 190 g | (3%) |
| Wheat flour: | 220 g | (3.5%) |

*In the copper*

| | | |
|---|---|---|
| Whitbread Goldings: | 55 g | (start of boil) |
| Fuggles hops: | 15 g | (last 15 minutes) |

*Typical characteristics*

| | | | |
|---|---|---|---|
| Brewing method: | C; Single infusion mash, top fermented | | |
| Mash liquor: | 15 litres | Alcohol content: | 5.5% |
| Mash temperature: | 66°C | Final gravity: | 1014 |
| Mash time: | 2 hours | Bitterness: | 27 EBU |
| Boil time: | 2 hours | Final volume: | 23 litres |

# Robinwood OLD FART

A rich, dark beer with stout-like character from the Robinwood brewery in West Yorkshire. Mouth filling mix of roast barley, raisins and sultanas with deep dry finish.

Classification:   English Bottle Conditioned Ale

Original gravity:          1060

*In the mash tun*

| | | |
|---|---|---|
| Pale malt: | 6,200 g | (90%) |
| Crystal malt: | 340 g | (5%) |
| Roast barley: | 340 g | (5%) |

*In the copper*

| | | |
|---|---|---|
| Whitbread Goldings: | 80 g | (start of boil) |
| Goldings hops: | 15 g | (last 15 minutes) |

*Typical characteristics*

| | | | |
|---|---|---|---|
| Brewing method: | C; Single infusion mash, top fermented | | |
| Mash liquor: | 16 litres | Alcohol content: | 6.1% |
| Mash temperature: | 66°C | Final gravity: | 1014 |
| Mash time: | 2 hours | Bitterness: | 40 EBU |
| Boil time: | 2 hours | Final volume: | 23 litres |

MALT EXTRACT VERSION – No mash required

Replace the pale malt with 4,550 grams of non-diastatic, medium coloured malt extract. Brew using Malt Extract Brewing – Method A.

# Theakston's OLD PECULIER

A dark and vinous old ale from Theakston's Masham brewery in North Yorkshire. Toffee and roast malt in the mouth; deep, bitter sweet finish with delicate hop underpinning.

Classification:   English Cask-Conditioned Old Ale

Original gravity:       1058

*In the mash tun*

| | | |
|---|---|---|
| Pale malt: | 4,500 g | (72%) |
| Crystal malt: | 620 g | (10%) |
| Black malt: | 120 g | (2%) |

*In the copper*

| | | |
|---|---|---|
| Maltose syrup: | 500 g | (8%) |
| Invert cane sugar: | 500 g | (8%) |
| Challenger hops: | 30 g | (start of boil) |
| Fuggles hops: | 35 g | (start of boil) |
| Fuggles hops: | 12 g | (last 15 minutes) |

*Typical characteristics*

| | | | |
|---|---|---|---|
| Brewing method: | C; Single infusion mash, top fermented | | |
| Mash liquor: | 13 litres | Alcohol content: | 6.2% |
| Mash temperature: | 66°C | Final gravity: | 1012 |
| Mash time: | 2 hours | Bitterness: | 30 EBU |
| Boil time: | 2 hours | Final volume: | 23 litres |

MALT EXTRACT VERSION – No mash required

Replace the pale malt with 3,300 grams of non-diastatic, medium coloured malt extract. Brew using Malt Extract Brewing – Method A.

# Wadworth's OLD TIMER

A heavy, aromatic winter beer – "ideal by a log fire" says the brewer. Full malt and fruit in the mouth, intense finish full of hop bitterness with banana and sultana notes.

*Classification:*   English Cask-Conditioned Winter Brew

Alcohol content:          1055

*In the mash tun*

| | | |
|---|---|---|
| Pale malt: | 5,350 g | (89%) |
| Crystal malt: | 180 g | (3%) |

*In the copper*

| | | |
|---|---|---|
| Invert cane sugar: | 480 g | (8%) |
| Fuggles hops: | 75 g | (start of boil) |
| Irish moss | 1 tsp | (last 15 minutes) |
| Goldings hops: | 5 g | (dry hops in cask) |

*Typical characteristics*

| | | | |
|---|---|---|---|
| Brewing method: | C; Single infusion mash, top fermented | | |
| Mash liquor: | 14 litres | Alcohol content: | 6.0% |
| Mash temperature: | 65°C | Final gravity: | 1011 |
| Mash time: | 2 hours | Bitterness: | 28 EBU |
| Boil time: | 2 hours | Final volume: | 23 litres |

MALT EXTRACT VERSION – No mash required

Replace the pale malt with 3,900 grams of non-diastatic, medium coloured malt extract. Brew using Malt Extract Brewing – Method A.

# Wiltshire OLD DEVIL

A powerful, sipping strong ale from the Wiltshire Brewery. Rich malt in the mouth offset by good, hoppy edge with complex finish of hop, fruit and nut.

*Classification:*   English Cask-Conditioned Old Ale

Original gravity:          1060

*In the mash tun*

| | | |
|---|---|---|
| Pale malt: | 4,650 g | (74%) |
| Crystal malt: | 190 g | (3%) |
| Amber malt: | 190 g | (3%) |
| Black malt: | 30 g | (0.5%) |

*In the copper*

| | | |
|---|---|---|
| Invert sugar: | 1,200 g | (19.5%) |
| Fuggles hops: | 40 g | (start of boil) |
| Goldings hops: | 35 g | (start of boil) |
| Goldings hops: | 15 g | (last 15 minutes) |

*Typical characteristics*

Brewing method:      C; Single infusion mash, top fermented.

| | | | |
|---|---|---|---|
| Mash liquor: | 13 litres | Alcohol content: | 7.1% |
| Mash temperature: | 66°C | Final gravity: | 1008 |
| Mash time: | 2 hours | Bitterness: | 30 EBU |
| Boil time: | 2 hours | Final volume: | 23 litres |

# 15 Explanatory Key to Recipes

*God bless the mother who gives birth to a brewer*　　　*Anon*

## General

All of the recipes contained herein are rather generous on ingredients to ensure that brewers at all levels of experience will get satisfactory results. It will also help to compensate for variations in ingredient quality. I am of the view that it is far less frustrating to end up with too much wort and having to throw some away than to end up with too little and having a beer that does not meet specification. There is nothing more disheartening to a beginner to find that he cannot achieve the results specified in the recipe. He blames his technique when nine times out of ten it is actually the recipe which is at fault.

All of the recipes have been designed assuming that a mash efficiency of 75 per cent will be achieved, which is a little on the low side; most people should be able to exceed it. I have also assumed that about 10 per cent wort loss will occur after all the syphoning and straining operations have taken place. The brewer should end up with 23 litres at the specified gravity.

Experienced brewers may find that they consistently end up with more wort than they can actually use and may need to reduce the quantities of the ingredients slightly for future brews.

## Original gravity

This is the original gravity published by the brewery concerned. All of the recipes have been designed to match the published gravity. The brewers' quoted gravities sometimes vary from one source to another. This is because they brew to an Excise gravity band and quote from the top, middle, or bottom of the band depending upon how the mood takes them. They could quote a 1040 bitter as 1038, 1040, or 1042.

## Ingredients

The ingredients for the copper and mash tun are shown separately to eliminate confusion for novice brewers. The percentage grist figures, calculated by weight of grist rather than extract contribution, are shown so that the knowledgeable brewer can estimate the quality of a particular beer. In many cases there was some guesswork in determining the ingredient ratios. Where glucose syrup and maltose syrup is called up, these refer to maize (corn) derived liquid brewing sugars. Any liquid brewing sugar will do.

## Brewing method

A, B and C refer to the three brewing methods, two malt extract, and one full mash described in the text.

## Mash liquor

Estimated quantity of mash liquor required. Not a particularly important parameter – it makes little difference. Use as much or as little mash liquor as you wish.

## Mash temperature
In all cases it is guessed but most brewers aim for about 66°C unless they are brewing something really special. If you maintain your mash temperature between about 62°C and 68°C you will get good results.

## Mash time
1½ – 2 hours. Not particularly critical.

## Boil time
1½ – 2 hours. A minimum of 1½ hours is required to achieve the calculated hop extraction efficiency. This figure was assumed when calculating the weights of hops required. The longer the boil the better the shelf life of the resulting beer.

## Alcohol content
This is percentage alcohol by volume. It is not the brewer's published ABV, but a computed version which reflects the home-brew version of the beer. The computed figure is surprisingly accurate and often matches the brewer's figure smack on, and is almost always within the 0.5 per cent tolerance that brewers are supposed to quote to. If anything, the computed figure is on the high side, particularly with dark beers, where a high proportion of black malt or roasted barley is used. This computed parameter has been invaluable in catching brewers who have not confessed to their brewing sugars and syrups.

## Final gravity
This has been computed; the breweries do not publish their final gravity. Not only is final gravity not the sort of thing that anyone would normally be interested in, but it also slowly drops with age as more dextrins are fermented.

## Bitterness
In EBUs, the standard method of assessing bitterness in beers. Some breweries provided the bitterness of their beers in European Bittering Units, others did not. Where the figure was supplied, it was used to calculate the quantity of hops required. When the figure was not supplied, it was estimated.

## Final volume
This is the estimated final volume after wort losses have been taken into account. This is the quantity that should end up in the barrel at the end of the day.

**Malt extract versions**
Most recipes have a malt extract version included; diastatic or non-diastatic extract has been specified as appropriate. Not all recipes have a malt extract version. Any recipe can be converted to a malt extract version by multiplying the amount of pale malt by 0.73 to give the quantity of malt extract required.

# 16 Glossary of Terms

*God blesse the Brewer, well cooled is my throate*        Barclay, 1530

**Adjunct**: The term applied to grain added to the grist which draws upon enzymes supplied by malt to convert starch into sugar. A material which does not draw upon these enzymes is not strictly speaking an adjunct.

**Aerobic respiration**: In our case, refers to the respiration of yeast (or bacteria) utilising air. Provides rapid yeast growth, but little alcohol is produced (see **anaerobic**)

**Alcohol**: In the brewing context refers to ethanol (ethyl alcohol).

**Ale**: A malt beverage fermented by a top working yeast.

**Alpha acid**: The hop resin humulon. A measure of the principal bittering substances present in hops.

**Amylase**: Alpha amylase and beta amylase are the enzymes responsible for the conversion of starch into sugars during the mash. Often referred to collectively as diastase.

**Anaerobic respiration**: In our case, refers to a form of respiration of yeast (or bacteria) which does not require the presence of air. Alcoholic fermentation by our yeast is only performed under anaerobic conditions.

**Attenuation**: The drop in specific gravity of the wort during the process of fermentation.

**Auxiliary finings**: A type of fining agent having the opposite ionic charge to primary finings and serves to drag protein out of suspension as opposed to yeast. Irish moss, or copper finings are a form of auxiliary finings.

**Back**: Pronounced "buck". Brewerspeak for a holding vessel. From the same etymology as the modern word bucket.

**Barley wine**: A strong ale.

**Barrel**: A 36-gallon cask. Brewer's standard unit of measurement.

**Batch fermentation**: The traditional method of brewing ale in individual batches.

**Beer**: Generic term for malt beverages. British brewers traditionally use the term beer, as opposed to ale, to refer to inferior products.

**Beta acid**: The hop resin lupulon.

**Beta glucan**: A gummy substance found in the aleurone layer of barley. Unmalted grains are rich in these gums. In moderation beta glucan aids beer foaming, but an excess could cause mash tun run-off problems.

**Bottom fermentation**: Bottom working refers to fermentation by a yeast which sits on the bottom of the fermentation vessel. Typical of lager yeasts.

**Burtonising**: Brewerspeak for the process of water treatment. Historically was the act of making the water similar to that of Burton-upon-Trent.

**Calcium bicarbonate**: The principal substance causing temporary hardness in our water supplies. A substantial quantity can be precipitated by boiling the water for a short period.

**Calcium sulphate**: The principal substance causing permanent hardness in our water supplies. Cannot be removed by boiling.

**Cask**: General term for all draught beer containers.

**Cask-conditioned beer**: Beer which conditions in the cask rather than in conditioning tanks at the brewery.

**Casting**: The act of emptying a vessel.

**Cereals**: Grain such as wheat, barley or maize used as malt adjuncts.

**Conditioning**: Maturation of beer after it leaves the fermenter.

**Copper**: The vessel in which the wort is boiled prior to fermentation. Referred to in the north of England as a kettle.

**Copper finings**: A substance, usually Irish moss, added to the copper during the boil to aid the protein break and improve the stability of the finished beer.

**Cracking**: The process of lightly crushing grain in order to expose the endosperm to the liquor during mashing.

**Dextrins**: The term given to non fermentable and slowly fermentable sugars remaining in the wort after fermentation. They provide residual sweetness and body.

**Diastase**: Old-fashioned collective name given to amylase group enzymes responsible for the conversion of starch into sugar during the mash.

**DMS**: Diastatic Malt Syrup, a malt extract that has a high level of enzymic activity which can be used to assist the conversion of adjuncts during a mash.

**Dropping**: In a brewery, is the process of transferring a fluid by the influence of gravity into another vessel, usually situated on the floor below.

**Dropping system**: A brewing method whereby the fermenting wort is dropped into a secondary vessel when it is about half-way through fermentation, leaving trub, hop debris, and surplus yeast behind.

**Dry hopping**: The act of adding a few hop cones to the beer after barrelling to add "hoppy" aroma.

**Enzyme**: A biological form of catalyst.

**Fining**: The practice of speeding or aiding the clearing of beer by adding colloidial or alginate type substances.

**Firkin**: A nine gallon cask.

**Gelatine**: A colloid derived from animal hooves, used as a fining agent in home brewing.

**Goods**: In brewerspeak, **grist** becomes **goods** when it is mixed with water in the **mash tun**.

**Grains**: Brewerspeak for spent **goods**.

**Green beer**: Beer that has not yet **matured**.

**Grist**: The mixture of milled malt and adjuncts waiting for the mash tun.

**Gyle**: A particular brew or batch of beer; a charge of the mash tun.

**Hogshead**: A 54-gallon cask.

**Hopback**: In a brewery, the vessel into which the wort is run after boiling to allow the spent hops and trub to settle. Trub is filtered out by the spent hops acting as a filter bed on the perforated floor.

**Hop extract**: Essential substances extracted from hops in a factory. Used extensively in home brew kits to eliminate a hop boil.

**Hot break**: The point at which the undesirable protein in the wort begins to precipitate out of solution during boiling.

**Initial heat**: The temperature at which **mashing** begins.

**Invert sugar**: The form of sucrose that breweries prefer to use. It is already inverted into its component parts of fructose and glucose, which saves the yeast having to do it. Brewers feel that invert sugar is not as prone to cause hangovers as is non-inverted sucrose.

**Irish Moss**: A substance often added to the copper as copper finings during the boil to aid the protein break and improve the stability of the finished beer. It is not a moss in fact, but a seaweed, carrageen (chondus crispus).

**Isinglass**: A rather mysterious **fining** agent made from the swim bladder of the sturgeon fish.

**Kilderkin**: An 18-gallon cask.

**Liquor**: Brewerspeak for brewing water.

**Malt extract**: A syrup made from malted barley that can be used as a short-cut method of brewing, ideal for beginners.

**Maltose**: Malt sugar

**Mashing**: The process of extracting fermentable sugars from malted grain by infusing it in water at a temperature of about 65°C.

**Maturation**: A period of time which should be allowed for the proper flavour of the beer to develop.

**Milling**: See **cracking**.

**Original gravity**: The gravity at which fermentation is begun.

**Parti-gyle**: In the modern sense applies when a whole range of beers are made from identical recipes, or from the same mash, the only difference being the amount of water added to the fermentation vessel.

**Ph**: A measure of the hydrogen ion content, and hence the acidity of a fluid.

**Pin**: A 4½-gallon cask.

**Pitching**: The act of introducing yeast into the fermentation vessel.

**Priming**: The act of adding sugar or wort to the barrels, to provide secondary fermentation and condition.

**Rack**: Brewerspeak for transferring a fluid leaving sediment behind, i.e. filling barrels with beer.

**Racking back**: Brewerspeak for a tank in which **green beer** is held for a short period before being transferred to the barrels.

**Racking gravity**: The specific gravity at which the **green beer** is put into barrels or bottles, usually a few degrees higher than **final gravity**.

**Rousing**: The process of stirring yeast into the beer in order to keep it in suspension. Sometimes refers to aerating the wort to maintain yeast activity.

**Run off**: The act of emptying a vessel, usually the mash tun.

**Secondary fermentation**: Process by which beer continues to ferment slowly and mature during conditioning.

**Shive**: Wooden bung with a penetrable centre core, fitted to beer casks. A porous wooden peg (spile) is driven through the centre to vent the cask.

**Skimming**: The act of removing surplus yeast from the surface of the wort during fermentation.

**Sparging**: The act of flushing valuable sugars from the **goods** in the mash tun.

**Square**: A rectangular vessel.

**Stillage**: A brick, wooden, or metal structure which supports casks of beer in the pub cellar.

**Strike heat**: The temperature of the mash **liquor** is before it meets the colder **grist**.

**Sweet wort**: The wort as collected from the mash tun before being boiled.

**Trub**: Undesirable protein matter precipitated during the boil.

**Ullage**: The empty space in a cask.

**Venting**: The act of allowing excess carbon dioxide to escape from a cask of beer prior to serving.

**Wort**: Pronounced "wurt". The sugary fluid which is extracted from malt in the mash tun.

# 17 Beers Index

*I view the tea drinking as a destroyer of health, an enfeebler of the frame, an engenderer of effeminacy and laziness, a debaucher of youth and maker of misery for old age....Thus he makes that miserable progress towards that death which he finds ten or fifteen years sooner than he would have found it if he had made his wife brew beer instead of making tea.*

William Cobbett, Cottage Economy, 1821

All the recipes are primarily designed for mashing from grain and every recipe in this book can be made in this manner. Use Brewing Method C if you are brewing from grain using a full mash.

Some recipes are suitable for brewing from malt extract and these are indicated thus:

(*) Indicates a recipe with a simple malt extract version where no mash is required. Suitable for novices. Non-diastatic malt extract should be used. Use brewing method A.

(-) Indicates a recipe with a malt extract version where a short mash is required in the boiler. These require the use of a diastatic malt extract such as EDME DMS, and should be brewed using Brewing Method B.

The recipes marked in this manner are simply a random selection and show the quantity of malt extract required as a footnote to the main recipe. This technique provides a wide range of recipes suitable for all levels of experience. Any recipe can be converted to a malt extract version, but remember that all major breweries actually use a full mash, not malt extract. See relevant text on the respective brewing methods and the explanatory key to recipes.

## MILD ALES                                                    Page

## PORTERS and STOUTS

## OLD ALES, STOCK ALES and BARLEY WINES

# 18 General Index

# 19 Conversions

*To cure a hangover:*

*Set a dish or platter of tynne upon the bare head filled with water, put an unce and halfe or two unces of melten lead therein whyle he hath it upon the head.*

*G.L. Gomme, The Gentlemen's Magazine, Vol 1. 1884*

One domestic (5ml) teaspoon holds the following approximate weights of the specified substances:

Calcium carbonate 3g
Citric acid 4g
Granulated sugar 6g
Irish moss 3g
Sodium bicarbonate 5.5g
Sodium metabisulphite 6g

A domestic teaspoon holds approximately: 5 ml.
A domestic dessert spoon holds approximately: 10 ml.
A domestic tablespoon holds approximately: 15 ml.
A large coffee mug holds approximately: 300 ml.

A half-pint beer mug holds approximately 16 grams of hops under light compression. A one pint beer mug holds about 33 grams of hops under moderate compression.

| 1 cubic metre | = | 33.315 cu ft. |
| | = | 219.98 Imperial gallons |
| | = | 264.18 US gallons |
| | = | 1000 litres |
| | = | 10 hl |
| | | |
| 1 Imp. gallon | = | 160 fluid ounces |
| | = | 1.2 US gallons |
| | | |
| 1 cubic foot | = | 6.25 Imperial gallons |
| 1 lb per gallon | = | 99.76 grams per litre (UK) |
| 1 brewer's barrel | = | 36 gallons (UK) |
| 1 brewer's quarter of barley | = | 448 lb (UK) |
| 1 brewer's quarter of malt | = | 336 lb (UK) |
| 1 lb per barrel | = | 2.77 grams per litre (UK) |

(A 20 lb per barrel wort would have a gravity 1055.4)

To convert:

| | | |
|---|---|---|
| Ounces to grams | Multiply by: | 28.35 |
| Pounds to kilograms | Multiply by: | 0.454 |
| Pints to litres | Multiply by: | 0.568 |
| Imp. gallons to litres | Multiply by: | 4.546 |
| US gallons to litres | Multiply by: | 3.785 |
| UK to US gallons | Multiply by: | 1.200 |

To convert the other way, divide by the figure shown.

1 kilogram = 1000 grams, 16 ounces = 1 lb

| | | | | | |
|---|---|---|---|---|---|
| 10 kg | = | 22 lb | 10 lb | = | 4.536 kg |
| 5 kg | = | 11 lb | 5 lb | = | 2.268 kg |
| 4 kg | = | 8 lb 13oz | 4 lb | = | 1.814 kg |
| 3 kg | = | 6 lb 9¾ oz | 3 lb | = | 1.361 kg |
| 2 kg | = | 4 lb, 6½ oz | 2 lb | = | 907g |
| 1 kg | = | 2 lb 3¼ oz | 1 lb | = | 454g |
| 500g | = | 1 lb 1½ oz | ½ lb | = | 227g |
| 250g | = | 8¾ oz | ¼ lb | = | 113g |
| 125g | = | 4½ oz | 1 oz | = | 28.4g |
| 100g | = | 3½ oz | ½ oz | = | 14.2g |
| 50g | = | 1¾ oz | ¼ oz | = | 7.1g |
| 25g | = | ¾ oz | ⅛ oz | = | 3.5g |

| | | | | |
|---|---|---|---|---|
| 25 litres | = | 5.5 imp gallons | = | 44 pints |
| 5 litres | = | 1.09 imp gallons | = | 8 pints, 16 fl. oz. |
| 4 litres | = | 0.88 imp gallons | = | 7 pints |
| 3 litres | = | 0.67 imp gallons | = | 5 pints, 5 fl. oz. |
| 2 litres | = | 0.44 imp gallons | = | 3 pints, 10 fl. oz. |
| 1 litre | = | 0.22 imp gallons | = | 1 pint, 15 fl. oz. |

Two books for every home brewer's shelf

## Home Brewing: The CAMRA Guide
*by Graham Wheeler*

The standard reference work for discerning home brewers – now thoroughly revised for a new edition with recipes for ales and lagers for full mash and malt extract brewing. £6.99.

## The Real Ale Drinker's Almanac
*by Roger Protz*

The book that unlocked the brewers' secrets and revealed for the first time the recipes for their beers. Invaluable for home brewers – the recipes, OGs and ABVs for every known cask-conditioned and bottle-conditioned ale brewed in Britain. Third edition, £6.99.

Available from book shops or direct from CAMRA, 34 Alma Road, St Albans, Herts AL1 3BW. Add £1 p&p per book. Access/Visa orders: 0727 867201.

## Join CAMRA!

Help the fight for good beer and pubs. CAMRA has 38,000 members organised countrywide, lobbying brewers and government.

Members get What's Brewing, CAMRA's national newspaper, free every month.
Big discounts on the annual Good Beer Guide and other CAMRA titles.

Free entry to CAMRA beer festivals.

Annual membership: £12/$20. Cheques to "CAMRA Ltd".

---

I wish to join CAMRA and agree to abide by the Memorandum and Articles of Association. I enclosed a cheque for £12/$20.

Name.....................................................

Address ................................................

.............................................................

............................ Post or Zip Code .........

Send to CAMRA,
34 Alma Road, St Albans, Herts AL1 3BW, Great Britain

---